THE MINISTRY OF A
BAPTIST
DEACON

A HANDBOOK FOR LOCAL CHURCH
SERVANT LEADERS

PAUL CHAPPELL

First published in 2010 by Striving Together Publications, a ministry of Lancaster Baptist Church, Lancaster, CA 93535. Striving Together Publications is committed to providing tried, trusted, and proven books that will further equip local churches to carry out the Great Commission. Your comments and suggestions are valued.

Striving Together Publications
4020 E. Lancaster Blvd.
Lancaster, CA 93535
800.201.7748

Cover design by Andrew Jones
Layout by Craig Parker
Edited by Monica Bass
Special thanks to our proofreaders

ISBN 978-1-59894-114-2

Printed in the United States of America

To the deacons of Lancaster Baptist Church.
Thank you for modeling the word *servant* as you
give tirelessly to our church family.

Table of Contents

ACKNOWLEDGEMENTS

I wish to thank the many deacons who have served our church family over the years. At the time of publication, Lancaster Baptist Church is celebrating our twenty-fifth year of ministry. Following are the deacons currently serving our church family:

John Alvarez	Ronald Harris	Miguel Sandoval
John Alvarez, Jr.	Dan Hartzell	Pete Seher
Rick Bishop	Steve Kellcr	Jamey Tanner
Jim Burns	Eldon Lofgren	John Teakell
Slade Carrizosa	Ed Marquez	JD Thorogood
Felix Dizon	David McCollum	Paul Tierney
Jerry Dunwoody	Alejandro Mendoza	Ron Weaver
Ken Elliott	Michael Michael	Bill Weible
Armando Garcia	Dan Migliore	Randy Wells
Scott Hand	Frank Quichocho	Cecil Whaley
Mark Hanna	Mahrous Rizkalla	Mike Yarborough

INTRODUCTION

Have you ever wished you could meet heroes of the past? What would it be like to rub shoulders with patriots and statesmen like George Washington, Patrick Henry, Daniel Webster, or Abraham Lincoln? Wouldn't you love to share a cup of coffee and glean a few moments of wisdom from preachers who moved their world for Christ like D.L. Moody or Charles Spurgeon?

What if you could share even just one day of missionary work with the Apostle Paul? Or listen to Peter preach? These apostles who led the early church were men whose ministry reached far beyond their own lives and time into our own.

There are seven other men, heroes of the first century, whom I look forward to meeting in Heaven. These men, less known than the apostles, gave of themselves for the furtherance of the Gospel in a unique way. Their ministry was one of service—to further the ministry of the apostles. Their names? *"Stephen...and Philip, and*

Prochorus, and Nicanor, and Timon, and Parmenas, and Nicolas..." (Acts 6:5).

These men, likely the first deacons, who Scripture records were *"full of faith and of the Holy Ghost"* are my heroes, and I thank God for them.

Actually, in many ways, I feel I've already met them—worked closely with them, in fact. I've had the privilege of sitting around a table with them several times a year, sharing the responsibilities of the church. I've watched them care for our church family and invest their whole heart into the work of God. They have participated with me in the vision, pressure, sacrifice, and labor of the ministry.

Pastors around the country have described similar men to me as well. It seems these pastors and the congregations they serve also benefit greatly from the ministry of their deacons.

A godly deacon is a great asset to the work of God. His servant leadership benefits the church in ways often unknown to most people. And his support and care for the pastor is invaluable.

As a pastor, I am deeply thankful for the ministry of a deacon. To the deacon who holds this book, I thank you for investing your life in the work of God and for giving of yourself in the service of God's people.

PART ONE

The Local Church Deacon

CHAPTER ONE

The Operation of the Church

As a young boy, I loved visiting the family farm in Colorado. Through the years, I spent hundreds of hours on the 4020 open cab tractor with Granddad, fascinated with the multitude of levers, shifts, and gauges surrounding me. As if it were second nature for him, Granddad always seemed to know exactly which button to push or gear to shift at the right time to keep the tractor operating smoothly.

Granddad took care of his tractor. It was a valuable piece of machinery to him—integral to farm production. When the day finally came that Granddad let me drive the tractor, he carefully instructed me in its operations. He didn't want a moment of carelessness to destroy his most necessary equipment.

A possession of far greater value to Christ than the tractor was to my Granddad is the local church. Christ's love for the church is seen in the great price He paid for it. Ephesians 5:25 tells us, *"Christ also loved the church, and gave himself for it."*

The church belongs to Christ. In Matthew 16:18 He declared, *"upon this rock I will build my church."* Christ purchased the church with His blood; He owns the church; and He has specified how it should operate.

As we will see in this chapter, Christ has appointed overseers and helpers to guide and aid the church in accomplishing its purposes, but foundational to understanding these offices is acknowledging that the Church belongs to Christ, and His authority is ultimate.

Jesus is the sole Proprietor, the Chief Shepherd, the Saviour, and the Sanctifier of the church. When we understand Christ's ownership, we can then follow His order in church operations.

What Is a Biblical Church?

When Scripture mentions the word *church*, it refers to a local, called out assembly of an organized body of believers who are saved and baptized. The very word translated *church* in the New Testament is *ecclesia*, which means "called out assembly." So a biblical church is a local, organized group of saved and baptized believers who have regular times of assembly and worship.

Local churches in the New Testament were organized bodies, not mere aggregations of people. Notice the following activities that denote organization:

• They received and dismissed members (Acts 9:26).

• They maintained worship and authority (Romans 16:17; Matthew 18:15–17).

• They managed affairs of the body (1 Corinthians 14:40).

A biblical church could be defined by the following:

Congregational Assembly: It is self-governing rather than being governed by outside leaders (Acts 16:5, 8:1; Matthew 18).

Theocratic Assembly: Every member is individually responsible to God, and each local church is directly responsible to God (Acts 15).

Christian Assembly: The people are obedient to the Bible and recognize that the body belongs to Christ (Hebrews 10:25; Acts 20:28).

Unlike Granddad's tractor, the local church is not to function simply as well-oiled machinery. It is a living organism comprised of people who need each other and corporately need and worship the Lord.

Yet, the church is also an organization with a specific purpose given from the Lord Himself. Successfully accomplishing that purpose requires organization—a structure for operation. In 1 Corinthians 14:40 Paul instructed the church at Corinth, *"Let all things be done decently and in order."*

So what is the order of operations for the church?

The first several chapters of Acts record the operation of the very first local church—the church at Jerusalem. Let's trace this church through some of its foundational experiences to understand the purpose of the church, discover how to overcome problems, and learn church polity.

The Purpose of the Church

The purpose of the church is summed up in the commission Christ gave His disciples just before He ascended to Heaven: *"And Jesus came and spake unto them, saying, All power is given unto me in heaven and in earth. Go ye therefore, and teach all nations, baptizing them in the name of the Father, and of the Son, and of the Holy Ghost: Teaching them to observe all things whatsoever I have commanded you: and, lo, I am with you alway, even unto the end of the world. Amen"* (Matthew 28:18–20).

This last command of Christ should be our highest priority; every facet of church activity should in some way relate to this, the purpose of the church. Acts 5:42 records that the Jerusalem church was indeed fulfilling this purpose: *"And daily in the temple, and in every house, they ceased not to teach and preach Jesus Christ."* This young church was constantly engaged in making the Gospel known to the world.

At Lancaster Baptist Church, we have emphasized this purpose in our three-point mission statement:

Loving God—Loving God begins in the heart, with a personal relationship with Him. As we gather and participate in Christ-honoring worship services and respond to the preaching of God's Word, this love flourishes. Mark 12:30 says, *"And thou shalt love the Lord thy God with all thy heart, and with all thy soul, and with all thy mind, and with all thy strength: this is the first commandment."*

Growing Together—We grow together, in Christ, through the study of God's Word. This occurs in our weekly services, in our smaller adult Bible classes, and in one-on-one discipleship.

Serving Others—We serve others as we find a place of ministry in the local body. We also serve by sharing the Gospel with those who need the Lord—through witnessing to friends, coworkers, neighbors, and loved ones, as well as in participating in church outreach and giving to missions.

As a church, our mission is to reach the world with the Gospel of Christ. We want to utilize every available biblical means, and we want to disciple and train every member to participate in accomplishing our church's purpose.

The Predicaments of the Church

As the Jerusalem church was diligently fulfilling its purpose, it wasn't long before problems arose: *"And in those days, when the number of the disciples was multiplied, there arose a murmuring of the Grecians against the Hebrews, because their widows were neglected in the daily ministration"* (Acts 6:1).

Our tendency is to view problems as a signal that the church is defunct, and certainly they can be indicators of needed adjustments. Notice, however, that the problems in the Jerusalem church arose when the *"number of the disciples was multiplied."* It was the growth of the church—not its insufficiency—that necessitated a solution.

The Jerusalem church now had thousands of people among their number, and with this growth came a need for more delegation of responsibilities. Any church that is growing will have challenges and complaints.

When problems arise within a church, they generally fall under the following categories:

Legitimate Concerns—Sometimes the concerns are legitimate questions that help the church. These concerns are need-oriented, as was the problem for the church at Jerusalem. The widows were being neglected, and the church was challenged to better care for the widows. This was a helpful issue with a proper response.

Preferential Concerns—Some issues that are raised in church life are preference-oriented. These might include the color of buses, the décor of buildings, or the location of classrooms. Preferential concerns are not a problem for a spiritually mature Christian. Mature Christians recognize these as non-essential to accomplishing the mission of the church and are willing to give deference to others where it helps the church move forward in fulfilling its purpose.

Carnal Concerns—These are aroused by carnal Christians who have ulterior motives and a hurtful spirit. John warned of such a man in 3 John 9, *"I wrote unto the church: but Diotrephes, who loveth to have the preeminence among them, receiveth us not."*

Carnal Christians who bring division to the church raise issues that become like a hurtful sore to the body: *"But shun profane and vain babblings: for they will increase unto more ungodliness. And their word will eat as doth a canker: of whom is Hymenaeus and Philetus"* (2 Timothy 2:16–17).

The damage of carnal issues usually begins with an uncontrolled tongue. James 3:5-6 says, *"Even so the tongue is a little member, and boasteth great things. Behold, how great a matter a little fire kindleth! And the tongue is a fire, a world of iniquity: so is the tongue among our members, that it defileth the whole body, and setteth on fire the course of nature; and it is set on fire of hell."*

From time to time, we experience forest fires here in Southern California. Several years ago, a small campfire was allowed to get out of control in the San Diego area, resulting in hundreds of thousands of acres being destroyed and the loss of lives and homes.

In a similar manner, carnal issues spreading through unbridled tongues within a church and a community damage countless lives— including young Christians and those who don't know the Lord. Innocent people who never began the issue are deeply affected by words not always spoken in a spirit of kindness.

Satanic Attacks—These are staged by those who would corrupt the doctrine or sabotage the biblical advancements of a church. Paul described them as "grievous wolves" in Acts 20:29–31, *"For I know this, that after my departing shall grievous wolves enter in among you, not sparing the flock. Also of your own selves shall men arise, speaking perverse things, to draw away disciples after them. Therefore watch, and remember, that by the space of three years I ceased not to warn every one night and day with tears."*

Although sometimes covered in sheep's clothing, these wolves are ruthless in their approach and brutal in their methods. Church leaders must warn their members of the dangers of false doctrines and the subverting people who promote them.

Problems are inherent to local church life because every church has people. It is important, however, that problems be addressed biblically so the purpose of the church might be accomplished.

It was in the context of answering a legitimate concern that would otherwise stifle the growth of the Jerusalem church that biblical polity of the church was given and incorporated. When this problem was solved by the appointment of deacons, the result was God-honoring: *"And the word of God increased; and the number of the disciples multiplied in Jerusalem greatly; and a great company of the priests were obedient to the faith"* (Acts 6:7).

The Polity of the Church

Polity is a form of government—the system by which an organized body functions. Scripture denotes two offices of church leadership—pastors and deacons. (Some denominations also believe in the role of elders, but Scripture indicates that the terms elder, bishop, and pastor refer to the same office. See 1 Peter 5:1–2; Acts 20:17, 28; Titus 1:5–7.)

It is the responsibility of the pastor to serve the church by leading, teaching, and overseeing the church work. It is the responsibility of deacons to serve the church family through assisting with care and the provision of special needs.

The office of the pastor

Perhaps the most democratic or congregational act of the church is the calling of a pastor. This is when a congregation seeks God's wisdom in whom He would have lead them as a church. Ephesians 4:11:–12 notes, *"And he gave some…pastors and teachers; For the perfecting of the saints, for the work of the ministry, for the edifying of the body of Christ."*

The church calls a pastor, and the pastor serves Christ by leading the church under Christ's authority. Notice the following ways the pastor serves the congregation:

He serves by leading. The church should be *led* by the pastor, not *run* by the pastor. Because the church belongs to Christ, the pastor must submit to Christ and to His Word.

He serves by overseeing. Acts 20:28 says, *"Take heed therefore unto yourselves, and to all the flock, over the which the Holy Ghost hath made you overseers, to feed the church of God, which he hath purchased with his own blood."* As an overseer, the pastor is to see the needs in the church and follow the Holy Spirit's leading in bringing order to the church.

He serves by shepherding. First Peter 5:2–4 compares the church to a flock of sheep of which Christ is the Chief Shepherd, and it compares the pastor to a shepherd leading the flock under the authority of Christ.

He serves by preaching. Paul admonished the young pastor Timothy, *"Preach the word; be instant in season, out of season; reprove, rebuke, exhort with all longsuffering and doctrine"* (2 Timothy 4:2). As noted next, this is one of the key roles of the pastor.

He serves by praying. The primary duties of a pastor given in Acts 6 are prayer and Bible study: *"Then the twelve called the multitude of the disciples unto them, and said, It is not reason that we should leave the word of God, and serve tables....But we will give ourselves continually to prayer, and to the ministry of the word"* (Acts 6:2, 4). The pastor best serves his church by being faithful in thorough study and diligent prayer for them.

The pastor is accountable to the Lord for his service to the church. Hebrews 13:17 tells us *"they watch for your souls, as they that must give account."* Some pastors enslave themselves to others' perception; this prohibits them from being able to please the Lord. But pastors who fear the Lord more than people are able to lead their people in obedience to the Lord.

Additionally, a pastor, like every other Christian, is accountable to other Christians. As a pastor, I've made a specific effort to keep accountability in all areas of my life—personal time, family, spiritual disciplines, finances, etc. There are several men, dear friends in the ministry, whom I ask to hold me accountable and have given permission to ask any questions they feel necessary. Although our natural tendency is to avoid accountability, I have found it to be invaluable in my life and ministry.

So, under Christ, the pastor is the leader, shepherd, and overseer of the church. But, as the Jerusalem church learned, the pastor needs the help of godly men to free him to give adequate time to prayer and study of the Word. Hence, God gave the church deacons to assist the pastor.

The office of the deacon

In the early establishing of the church at Jerusalem, the church recognized the need for filling the office of deacons.

> Then the twelve called the multitude of the disciples unto them, and said, It is not reason that we should leave the word of God, and serve tables. Wherefore, brethren, look ye out among you seven men of honest report, full of the Holy Ghost and wisdom, whom we may appoint over this business. But we will give ourselves continually to prayer, and to the ministry of the word. And the saying pleased the whole multitude: and they chose Stephen, a man full of faith and of the Holy Ghost, and Philip, and Prochorus, and Nicanor, and Timon, and Parmenas, and Nicolas a proselyte of Antioch.—ACTS 6:2–5

These first deacons were godly men with servant's hearts. We'll explore their role and responsibilities more thoroughly throughout the rest of this book.

The People of the Church

If the pastor is to lead the church, and the deacons are to serve the church, what is the role of the people? Quite simply, the people *are* the church! God never intended the church to be run by the pastor and the deacons. Rather these men equip the church to accomplish the purpose God has given.

Throughout Acts and the epistles, we see various responsibilities of the people of the church:

Pray for one another—Acts 2
Acknowledge and care for the pastor—1 Timothy 5:17; Hebrews 13:7
Love one another—1 Corinthians 13
Study Scripture—2 Timothy 2:15
Refrain from gossip—2 Thessalonians 3:11–12
Pursue holiness—1 Peter 1:16
Bear each others' burdens—Galatians 6
Give to the Lord's work—2 Corinthians 9:6–8
Witness to the lost—Acts 1:8

Several years ago, a man moved to our area from a different state. He visited our church and inquired about becoming a member. As I explained the polity of our church to him (led by the pastor, served by the deacons, and participated in by members), he breathed a sigh of relief. Then he explained, "At my old church, our monthly business meetings could have been better called 'congregational debates.' It seemed that every month trivial issues were discussed and argued—to the point that it was distracting to my faith."

The operational roles that Christ has given to the church help us reach our great purpose—to know Christ and to make Him known. Although every church will have problems arise, when we follow God's blueprint, we will have fewer interruptions as we work together for the cause of Christ.

CHAPTER TWO

The Office of a Deacon

A ny pastor can attest to the fact that there is too much work to be done in a church by one man. When a pastor is called to a church, he is called to equip the saints for the work of the ministry (Ephesians 4:12).

As we saw in our last chapter, this responsibility will primarily be accomplished through preaching God's Word. There are so many day-to-day tasks that must be taken care of in the ministry that if the pastor had no help, he would neglect his greatest duty—making sure he is spiritually prepared to preach through study, prayer, and time alone with God.

For this reason, the early church leaders appointed godly men from out of the congregation to help them in the daily administration over the church's affairs.

The Bible word for deacon is primarily translated "servant" or, "one selected by the people and charged with the temporal affairs of the local congregation." Thus, the primary role as a Baptist deacon is to serve the pastor and church.

The Lord Jesus Christ is our ultimate example of a servant. Over and over again in the New Testament, we see Him meeting the everyday needs of common people—food, healing, money, friendship, hope, and encouragement.

Acts 6:3 provides the list of what the apostles were looking for in their selection of the first deacons: *"Wherefore, brethren, look ye out among you seven men of honest report, full of the Holy Ghost and wisdom, whom we may appoint over this business....And the saying pleased the whole multitude: and they chose Stephen, a man full of faith and of the Holy Ghost, and Philip, and Prochorus, and Nicanor, and Timon, and Parmenas, and Nicolas a proselyte of Antioch"* (Acts 6:3, 5).

Notice the following characteristics of these men:

They had a godly influence—The apostles instructed the church *"look ye among you."* The men chosen had already exerted a godly influence that was noticed in the church—*before* they were given a position of church leadership.

They had godly relationships—The words *"among you"* note their ability to relate and get along with others. In addition to a right vertical relationship with the Lord, they had proper horizontal relationships with their church family.

They had a godly reputation—These were men of *"honest report."* They were men of integrity and honor, men whom the church could trust.

They were full of wisdom—These were not spiritual "wannabes." They were men who walked with God, yielded to the Holy Spirit, and were full of godly wisdom.

They had a servant's heart—The initial job given to these men was to serve the church widows. This was not a glamorous job description, yet these men were chosen because of their willingness to serve.

They were men of faith—Because the pastor is the overseer of the church, the men who serve with him must have faith to follow their pastor. Some Christians seem to have the mind-set that a qualification of a deacon is to "stand up to the pastor." I thank the Lord for the faith of our deacons at Lancaster Baptist Church who are willing to follow my faith (Hebrews 13:7). When I share with our deacons the vision the Lord has placed on my heart, rather than quibbling over whether or not we should move forward, they set to work in making plans for how it can be best accomplished. Their hearts of faith have contributed greatly in allowing our church to reach our community with the Gospel.

After the selection of the first seven deacons, Acts 6 focuses on the life of one of these men—Stephen. As the only expanded biography of a deacon in Scripture, Stephen's life models the characteristics of a godly deacon.

> And Stephen, full of faith and power, did great wonders and miracles among the people. Then there arose certain of the synagogue, which is called the synagogue of the Libertines, and Cyrenians, and Alexandrians, and of them of Cilicia and of Asia, disputing with Stephen. And they were not able to resist the wisdom and the spirit by which he spake. Then they suborned men, which said, We have heard him speak blasphemous words against Moses, and against God. And they stirred up the people, and the elders, and the scribes, and came upon him, and caught him, and brought him to the council, And set up false witnesses, which said, This man ceaseth not to speak blasphemous words against this holy place, and the law: For we have heard him say, that this Jesus of Nazareth shall destroy this place, and shall change the customs which Moses delivered us. And all that sat in

*the council, looking stedfastly on him, saw his face as it had been the face of an angel.—*ACTS 6:8–15

He was full of faith.

The Christian's journey is begun in faith when he trusts Christ alone for his salvation. Yet God intends that this infant-like faith expand and grow as we come to Christian maturity. Colossians 2:6 instructs, *"As ye have therefore received Christ Jesus the Lord, so walk ye in him."* Stephen's life was characterized by faith.

Of more importance to the church than a deacon being well-versed in business or equipped with financial wisdom is that he is full of faith. Moving forward for the cause of Christ, as every church desires to do, requires a series of faith steps: *"For we walk by faith, not by sight"* (2 Corinthians 5:7). When deacons are *"full of faith,"* the church is encouraged to advance for Christ under the leadership of the pastor.

He was full of power.

Stephen's life was full of power because he was full of the Holy Spirit. Zechariah 4:6 tells us that it is only by God's Spirit that God's work can be accomplished: *"Then he answered and spake unto me, saying, This is the word of the LORD unto Zerubbabel, saying, Not by might, nor by power, but by my spirit, saith the LORD of hosts."*

Deacons who are fully yielded to the Lord and follow the leading of the Holy Spirit in their lives can open the floodgates of God's power to bless their church and to impact the world through their church.

He was filled with the Word.

That Stephen was a diligent student of God's Word is evident in his sermon recorded in Acts 7. Even under tremendous pressure, he was able to recall Scripture and present it to his accusers with concise clarity. He preached that Jesus Christ had fulfilled the pictures of the Old Testament ceremonies, and he understood the importance of the New Covenant (or church age).

As a deacon, Stephen had a biblical understanding of the church and Christian worship that surpassed many others. His life and later legacy as the first Christian martyr encouraged his church to better fulfill their purpose of the great commission. His testimony had a direct bearing on the salvation of the Apostle Paul, one of the most vehement persecutors of the early church.

A deacon who is full of faith, power, and the Word of God is an incredible blessing to his church and pastor.

Following this three-fold description of Stephen's life, Scripture provides a real-time view of his life, demonstrating how these characteristics impacted his ministry.

He faced spiritual opposition.

Every man who stands to speak the truth in God's power will face spiritual opposition. This is why Paul instructed Christians to stand firm in the armor of God:

> *Finally, my brethren, be strong in the Lord, and in the power of his might. Put on the whole armour of God, that ye may be able to stand against the wiles of the devil. For we wrestle not against flesh and blood, but against principalities, against powers, against the rulers of the darkness of this world, against spiritual wickedness in high places. Wherefore take unto you the whole armour of God, that ye may be able to withstand in the evil day, and having done all, to stand.*—EPHESIANS 6:10–13

For Stephen, this opposition came from the synagogue of the Libertines—a group of Jews who had been dispersed outside of Israel and now gathered in Jerusalem to worship. Their apologists were unable to argue Stephen's knowledge of the Old Testament Scriptures which pointed the way to Christ. This again emphasizes the necessity of Bible study. Every deacon should be able to articulate and defend the basic doctrines of the Gospel.

These men hired informants to falsely accuse Stephen of blasphemy. The charges against him were so fierce that the strongest passions of the Jewish people were raised. Yet, even then, Stephen was *"stedfast, unmoveable…abounding in the work of the Lord"* (1 Corinthians 15:58) as he witnessed of Christ to his accusers.

He had grace under pressure.

The fullness of grace that Stephen exhibited indicated that he was a Christ-like man. Without compromising truth, Stephen proclaimed the Gospel with a grace that reflected his Saviour. John 1:14 describes Christ as *"full of grace and truth."*

Grace does not demand a lack of truth, nor does truth demand a lack of grace. A deacon who, through spending time with Christ, learns to balance the two is a great asset to Gospel ministry.

He displayed the presence of Christ.

All who gathered to watch the spectacle of Stephen's accusation and martyrdom saw neither hate nor horror in his countenance. Instead, they *"looking stedfastly on him, saw his face as it had been the face of an angel."*

Those who serve others will be mistreated. Although most deacons today do not expect to suffer the degree of abuse Stephen endured, there will be times when they will be misunderstood, misrepresented, or mistreated by others—within and without the church.

Vance Havner once said, "We need men of the cross, with the message of the cross, bearing the marks of the cross."

So we learn from the description of the first deacons that this office should be filled with men who desire to serve their church and are engaged in witnessing for Christ. Each of the seven men chosen in Acts 6 were first godly Christians before they were appointed as deacons.

We glimpsed in the life of Stephen a portrait of a godly Christian deacon. His life was full of faith, power, and Scripture, enabling him to declare the truth with grace, even under pressure and to display the presence of Christ at all times.

In the next chapter, we'll see the specific qualifications Scripture gives for the selection of deacons.

CHAPTER THREE

The Qualifications of a Deacon

If you needed to employ someone, what qualifications would you look for? Experience? Training? Skill? Teachability? Really, the necessary qualifications would depend on the job at hand. The more crucial the job, the more stringent the qualifications.

The office of a deacon is a holy office—one of only two biblically established offices in the church. Because of its sanctity, God's requirements for deacons are high.

> *Likewise must the deacons be grave, not doubletongued, not given to much wine, not greedy of filthy lucre; Holding the mystery of the faith in a pure conscience. And let these also first be proved; then let them use the office of a deacon, being found blameless. Even so must their wives be grave, not slanderers, sober, faithful in all things. Let the deacons be the husbands of one wife, ruling their children and their own houses well.*—1 TIMOTHY 3:8–12

So, God's qualifications for deacons include the following:

Grave—This describes a man who understands the seriousness of his ministry and gives reverence to spiritual ministry. Grave men can also be joyful men, but they will not be characterized by a flippant or silly attitude.

Not doubletongued—A double-tongue is one of deceit and hypocrisy. Rather than highly esteeming truth, it speaks that which is convenient to a given setting. A deacon must be a man of his word, a man who can be trusted with confidential information.

A double-tongue also implies gossiping, back-biting, undermining, or holding grudges. These greatly hinder the work of God and disqualify a man from the office of deacon.

Not given to much wine—Deacons should be especially careful to abstain from harmful substances that would tend to weaken the testimony of their church (1 Thessalonians 5:22). This would include the use of intoxicating liquors, drugs, or tobacco. They should never bring disrepute on the church through sinful addictions or associations.

Not greedy of filthy lucre—Proverbs warns of the danger of leadership who will be bribed or alter their convictions for personal gain (Proverbs 17:23; 19:29). Greed twists minds and hinders sound judgment. A deacon controlled by the love of money can promote a competitive, mercenary-like spirit in the church.

Additionally, a deacon who is controlled by the love of money prohibits himself from being available to serve. Financial success is not sinful; however, if a man is constantly involved in overtime hours or lives at his office, he will struggle with being faithful to church and finding time to serve the church family.

This qualification of a deacon would also indicate that they are generous givers. Matthew 6:21 explains, *"For where your treasure is, there will your heart be also."* Financially investing in the work of the church through tithes and offerings increases one's heart-felt support for the ministries of his church.

Holding the mystery of the faith in a pure conscience— "The mystery of the faith" refers to the Gospel of Christ. The deacon who holds the Gospel in a pure conscience is a man who has a clear grasp on biblical truth and consistently passes it on to others. He is both a student and a teacher of Scripture.

When Paul bid farewell to the leaders at Ephesus, he was able to do so with the claim of a pure conscience: *"Wherefore I take you to record this day, that I am pure from the blood of all men. For I have not shunned to declare unto you all the counsel of God"* (Acts 20:26–27). Because Paul was faithful in soulwinning and diligent in discipleship, he had a conscience pure of guilt toward other men. This is the standard of ministry we should each desire in our churches.

Proved—The office of a deacon should not be treated as a position of discipleship. The requirements given for deacons should already be established in a man's life *before* he is appointed to this office. Although every Christian should seek continued spiritual growth, a deacon must be proven in his spiritual maturity to hold the office. To appoint baby Christians to this leadership is detrimental to their growth and deprives the church of the leadership it needs.

Blameless—As Samuel ended his ministry as a judge in Israel, his testimony was so blameless that he was able to stand before an entire nation and ask if he had defrauded any person (1 Samuel 12:3–5). This level of integrity is an absolute necessity in church leaders. There should not be one person in the church who can accurately accuse a deacon of a dishonest transaction. The tragedy of embezzlement in a church can only happen when this requirement of a pure conscience is not in place.

The lifestyles of a deacon and his family should be godly and above reproach. His testimony should be sterling, pointing others to Christ and adding to the positive testimony of his church in the community.

Even so must their wives...—We'll more closely examine the role of deacons' wives in chapter 7, but for now, we'll note that they must meet the same qualifications as their husbands up to this point—*"grave, not slanderers, sober, faithful in all things."*

Church leadership, in many ways, opens a man's home to scrutiny. Indeed, the very fact that he has been appointed to leadership is a statement that he is worthy of being an example to others. For this reason, his wife must share the same godly testimony and heart for service as her husband.

The husband of one wife—This wording literally refers to a "one-woman man." It means that he is first of all married, and secondly married to one wife only. In addition to prohibiting polygamous or divorced men from the office, this phrase also speaks to the purity of a man's sexual life. He must not be involved with any woman other than his wife in any way—through affairs, pornography, or emotional attachments. He must be completely committed to his wife and live in personal purity.

Ruling their children and their own houses well—The deacon must first be a spiritual leader in his home before he can be a spiritual leader in the church. His children, of course, will not be perfect, but their spirits and countenances should reflect a godly and nurturing home environment.

Faithful in all things—Although specifically applied to the deacon's wife, this phrase sums up all the qualifications of both the deacon and his wife. They should be solid Christians, faithful to the Lord and their church.

This faithfulness should include attendance to the regular and special services of the church—Sunday services, midweek Bible study, revival meetings, deacons meetings, and other special meetings. Deacons should attend regular soulwinning meetings and be faithful in soulwinning and visitation, practicing 2 Timothy 2:2.

First Timothy 3:13 says, *"For they that have used the office of a deacon well purchase to themselves a good degree, and great boldness in the faith which is in Christ Jesus.*" I thank the Lord for our deacons at Lancaster Baptist Church who use *"the office of a deacon well"* by recognizing the stewardship of their influence. It is a delight to see their faithfulness to the Lord and to their families. It is a joy to watch them serve by mentoring younger Christians in discipleship and soulwinning.

The high qualifications for deacons point to the fact that testimony counts. People closely observe church leadership and will seldom rise to a higher level of spiritual maturity. No one has reached a plateau of perfection, but deacons should maintain a blameless testimony and obvious heart for growth and grace.

The Effective Servant Leader

If you were to visit Lancaster Baptist Church, you would likely be greeted warmly by several of our deacons. As ushers, Sunday school teachers, and later with a follow-up visit, the deacons are gracious hosts making visitors feel welcomed and appreciated.

But you would never guess that your welcomers were deacons, for they serve with a humble spirit focused on others' needs rather than on their own position. They will never introduce themselves citing their position and tenure as a deacon.

Our church is blessed with deacons who are willing to serve in any capacity—even in the mundane and tedious jobs. When a need arises, our deacons are the first to respond, but they don't attempt to "pull rank" or receive recognition. In short, they are servant leaders.

Jesus stated, "...*Ye know that they which are accounted to rule over the Gentiles exercise lordship over them; and their great ones exercise authority upon them. But so shall it not be among you:*

but whosoever will be great among you, shall be your minister: And whosoever of you will be the chiefest, shall be servant of all. For even the Son of man came not to be ministered unto, but to minister, and to give his life a ransom for many" (Mark 10:42–45).

Servant leadership was Jesus' idea. The word *minister* literally means "to attend to or to wait upon." Jesus took on Himself the *"form of a servant"* (Philippians 2:7). No greater example of service could ever be seen than that of Jesus Christ. He is the ultimate display of servant leadership.

As a deacon, it is vital that you view your office as that of a servant leader. Your perspective on this principle will play out in every facet of your leadership—both in personal settings and in church ministry. This concept is a deep heart-level trait rooted in how you perceive your position in Christ.

If we were to ask Jesus, "how should we view this role," His simple answer would be "as servant of all." He taught us to minister—to give ourselves as He gave Himself. He exemplified a kind of leadership that is foreign to secular corporations or government hierarchies. He introduced a "towel and bowl" kind of leadership—the kind of leadership where the Creator of the universe stoops to wash the dirty feet of His creation. This is the kind of leadership where the God of all power and glory gives His life to save the souls of fallen men who have rejected Him—the kind of leadership that gains by giving, lives by dying, and rises by kneeling.

Becoming an undershepherd

A shepherd personifies the heart of a servant leader. His chief ambition is not recognition or comfort; it is the well-being of his flock. Although King, Christ called Himself "the Good Shepherd," one who gives His very life for the sheep (John 10:11). In Him, we see a true King kneeling to wash His disciples' feet. We see the King of kings serving men, loving people, and living among those to whom He ministered.

The Chief Shepherd of the church is Christ Himself, and pastors serve as shepherds under the authority of Christ as they lead and feed the flock (1 Peter 5:3–4). Like a shepherd, the pastor cares deeply for the flock and gives himself in ways they will never know for their spiritual growth and health.

Deacons who develop the heart of an undershepherd increase their ability to assist their pastor and serve their church. Rather than seeing their office as a position demanding respect, they see their role as a servant of the church. They rejoice, not when they are honored for their investments, but when their investments bear fruit in the lives of others. They serve without limits and find their joy in the success of those whom they serve. This is servant leadership, and this is the model of leadership every church needs in their deacons.

The *office* of the deacon is a high and holy call, but the *role* of a deacon is one of lowliness and humility. Your *purpose* is the grand, eternal purpose of Almighty God, but your *function* is one of Christlike understatement.

In Jesus we do not see one with lavish appointments, extensive entourages, and a luxurious lifestyle. Even though He was worthy of that, He chose to live a serving life. He is called the King of kings, but He called Himself the Son of man. He is called the Lord of lords, but He never lorded over anyone. His greatness and power and love were exemplified and displayed through simple obedience to His Heavenly Father and through steadfast compassion upon all He touched.

If you perceive your role as one requiring special recognition and privileges, your heart will become lifted up, your spirit self-absorbed, and your God will become distant—actually resisting your "kingly" efforts "*...for God resisteth the proud, and giveth grace to the humble*" (1 Peter 5:5). Yet, if you see yourself as Christ saw Himself, you will live in humility, thereby freeing the mighty hand of God to bless your service and "*exalt you in due time*" (1 Peter 5:6).

The ministry of a servant leader

Yours is a call to minister—to serve. That ministry will involve labor and hard, sometimes tedious, work. God established the very office of the deacon to absorb some of the labor necessary for the church to function. A servant leader is not afraid to get his hands dirty, work hard, or exhaust himself for his Master, and he doesn't demand recognition for his investment.

Consider the great "kenosis" passage where Jesus completely emptied Himself and became obedient to the will of His Father:

> *If there be therefore any consolation in Christ, if any comfort of love, if any fellowship of the Spirit, if any bowels and mercies, Fulfil ye my joy, that ye be likeminded, having the same love, being of one accord, of one mind. Let nothing be done through strife or vainglory; but in lowliness of mind let each esteem other better than themselves. Look not every man on his own things, but every man also on the things of others. Let this mind be in you, which was also in Christ Jesus: Who, being in the form of God, thought it not robbery to be equal with God: But made himself of no reputation, and took upon him the form of a servant, and was made in the likeness of men: And being found in fashion as a man, he humbled himself, and became obedient unto death, even the death of the cross.*—PHILIPPIANS 2:1–8

The motives of a servant leader

Spiritual servants do not seek status; they seek the mind of Christ. Success is a moving target, but leadership is a fixed goal. In spiritual leadership, Jesus—His glory, His pleasure, and His purpose—is the goal. A servant leader is motivated not by a personal agenda or self-gratification, but by the lifting up of Jesus Christ. John the Baptist said, *"He must increase, but I must decrease"* (John 3:30).

This is the kind of leader that God entrusts with influence, and it is the kind of leader that God's people can follow with willing-hearted sincerity.

The methods of a servant leader

A servant leader will boldly proclaim the truth of God, but he will do so with a spirit of sincere love and humility. Stephen's message in Acts 7 is a perfect example of this balance of boldness and humility. A local church deacon must be able to be firm in biblical positions while at the same time exhibiting grace and demonstrating sincere love to those whom he serves.

The Apostle Paul made two declarations in 1 Thessalonians 2. He said first that he was bold to speak the Gospel, and he then stated that he spoke without guile, only with Christ-centered, pure motives. What a wonderful blend of Holy Spirit boldness and a Christlike servant's heart.

The role of a spiritual leader is one of servant leadership. In a world where men are climbing political and corporate ladders— where men seek to enthrone themselves by using the worship of others—we are called to humbly lead men to the worship of Christ.

Some men might argue, "If I take that kind of servant role, people will 'walk all over me.'" Yes. That's what they did to Jesus. It's called "being used"!

In the following chapter, we'll examine specific duties often attended to by deacons. These ministries, however, can only be God-honoring as they are performed by men with servants' hearts and a passion to see Christ exalted—servant leaders willing to spend and be spent for Christ and His church.

CHAPTER FIVE

The Duties of a Deacon

Although Scripture provides no list of duties for deacons, it is not difficult to locate such a list in the needs of a local church. The first deacons found their "to do" list in the pressing need of widows lacking care. These men were asked to fill the need, and they quickly shouldered the responsibility. We might surmise that they were not long in finding other areas of ministry as well.

Because of the variety of ministries and needs of individual churches and pastors, the duties of deacons will be considerably different from one location to the next. Whatever the specifics, however, the job description remains the same—servant.

At Lancaster Baptist Church, our deacons serve in several vital capacities:

- Ministry to widows
- Ministry to the needy

- Altar counseling
- New Member welcoming and integration
- Funerals
- Serving the Lord's Table
- Offering count
- Administrative committees

Practical helps for some of these ministries will be given in the second part and appendices of this book, but below is a brief description of the deacon's role in several of these ministries at Lancaster Baptist Church.

Undershepherd program

Through the Undershepherd Program of Lancaster Baptist Church, each deacon is assigned a group of members based on alphabetic division. Thus, he assists the "undershepherd" or pastor in his mission. A list of assigned members is given to each deacon annually, and is then updated monthly. The deacon is responsible to visit these members at a time of death, bereavement, or serious illness. Additionally, the birthdates of these families are shared with the deacon and his wife, who may send birthday and anniversary cards to those on their list.

This program, combined with the efforts of the pastoral care ministry and adult Bible class care groups, helps to insure that no one is forgotten during a time of difficulty or sickness.

Ministering to the widows

One of the primary functions of the first century deacons was to minister to the needs of widows. In addition to the Undersheperd lists, the deacons of Lancaster Baptist Church are given two or three widows who are to be given special care. The widows are not necessarily assigned alphabetically, but care is given to spread them evenly among the deacons. This ministry may include a phone call to give a word of encouragement, visits to the home or hospital, and home repairs (such as replacing water heaters, or garbage disposals). If the item of service needed for a widow is something that can be accomplished easily, the deacon will normally take care of it himself. If it requires professional labor, such as a certified plumber, the deacon will notify the church financial administrator and arrangements are made for the widow's need to be met. We believe that serving the widows in this fashion is honoring to the Lord and consistent with the principles found in Acts 6.

Ministering to the needy

The primary objective of the church is to fulfill our Lord's Great Commission: to win, baptize, and train people for Christ. In the process of carrying out this work, however, there are many other duties the pastor and deacons face each week.

One such duty is to compassionately help those who are in need of physical and financial assistance. A person's greatest need is the salvation of his soul. Therefore, before any assistance is given, the deacons endeavor to give the Gospel to the needy person.

On a rotating basis, the deacons stand in the lobby after the church services to help the pastor with needs of the church family as well as others who may ask for financial assistance. (See Appendix 6 for assistance guidelines.)

The pastor and pastoral staff deal daily with these types of needs; the deacons, however, can help fulfill this role in and around service times to allow the pastoral staff to more effectively lead, direct, and guide the overall flock of the church. Special situations and questions may be directed to the pastor during the regular meetings or at other times, should a need be of an urgent nature.

Funerals

Romans 12:15 admonishes, *"Rejoice with them that do rejoice, and weep with them that weep."* Times of loss, such as funerals, are an opportunity for deacons to sympathize with and comfort church members who are mourning.

The deacons of Lancaster Baptist Church play a tremendous role in executing funerals for church members or immediate loved ones of church members. While the pastoral staff and adult class leaders are intricately involved in ministering to the family, the deacons are asked to pray for, visit, and care for the family, and attend the funeral, if possible.

The deacons, along with their wives, are also asked to coordinate meals for the family as well as the family reception following the funeral.

New member welcoming

New church members should immediately know they are a vital part of the church and a valued member of their new church family. At Lancaster Baptist Church, deacons help oversee the welcoming of new members.

New Members Class—Several times throughout the year, I teach a new members class on four consecutive Sundays during the Sunday school hour. Our adult teachers encourage new or prospective church members to attend the class for these weeks.

This class has been incredibly successful as it has given new members an early chance to bond with me as their pastor, have their questions answered, understand our discipleship program, and establish in their minds and hearts what our church teaches and what is expected of them as new members. Additionally, it has encouraged prospective members to join.

In the four week class, we cover the following topics:

1. The Story of Lancaster Baptist Church
2. The Beliefs of Lancaster Baptist Church
3. The Structure of Lancaster Baptist Church
4. Life in the Family of Lancaster Baptist Church

As we begin each class, I often introduce the students to one of our deacons and his wife so they may better know who is available to serve them. At times, deacon couples have hosted the classes with light refreshments.

New Members Reception—A welcome for new members of the church is held after the last week of the new members class. Following the Sunday evening service, I call the new members to the front of the auditorium and introduce them to the church family. The church family is then encouraged to meet in the fellowship area immediately following the service to introduce themselves to the new members and enjoy a cake reception and time of fellowship. The deacons and their wives and staff are encouraged to greet the new members at this reception.

The deacons and their wives help prepare for and host these receptions. To involve other members, we ask deacons' wives to not bring the cakes themselves, but to recruit other ladies in this ministry. Part of the discipleship process is teaching young Christians to have hearts to serve and providing opportunities to be a blessing.

Preferably, newer members will be asked to bring the cake, as this is a great ministry for their immediate involvement and is one which they enjoy. (Brand new members, of course, should not be asked to bring a cake to their own reception.)

New Members Packets—Each new member of Lancaster Baptist Church is given a New Members packet containing several items that we believe are relevant to new members, including the church calendar, giving envelopes and information about our church polity and doctrine. The deacons are asked to deliver these packets to new members within a few weeks of membership.

The deacon is encouraged to make a visit to the home of the new member, perhaps with his wife. They sit down with the new member, welcome the new member to the church, express the love of the pastor, explain the items in the New Members packet, and ask if the new member has any questions. Each packet contains the following items:

- Calendar
- Church constitution
- Bible reading schedule
- Lancaster Baptist Church financial policy
- Tithe envelopes
- Lancaster Baptist School brochure (if applicable)
- Discipleship interest form
- Gideons enrollment card
- *The Trail of Blood* pamphlet
- *Why Baptists Are Not Protestants* book
- Ministry survey/spiritual gifts test
- *Your Pastor and You* book
- *Charismatic Confusion* booklet
- Dailyintheword.org enrollment card
- *What is a Biblical Fundamentalist?* book
- Statement of doctrine and philosophy
- *Living on God's Economy* book
- Lifestages brochure (listing our adult Bible classes)
- Wednesdays in the Word brochure (describing our midweek Bible study)

A report form is attached to the front of each New Members packet. After delivering a packet, the deacon is asked to indicate on the form that the packet was delivered and return it to the church office.

By early welcoming and serving new members, deacons have greater immediate and future opportunities to minister to these new families in the church.

Committees

Although Lancaster Baptist Church does not officially have functioning committees for the purpose of ministry operations, the deacons do formulate select committees to serve the congregation and the pastor more effectively. Committee work provides an opportunity to serve in a specific function for the purpose of allowing the pastor more time to study and pray. The pastor is a de facto member of all committees.

Listed below are the committees presently formed by the deacons of the church (detailed descriptions of each committee are in Appendix 4):

1. Building, Safety, and Expansion Committee
2. Legal Committee
3. Missions Committee
4. School Committee
5. College Committee
6. Lord's Table Committee
7. Discipline Committee
8. Finance Committee
9. Audit Committee
10. Compensation Committee

These committees are not a separate office and are created by the pastor based on perceived ministry needs. Committees are changed, and members are re-assigned from time to time. Items related to each of these committees may be discussed in the monthly deacons meetings.

Monthly meetings and reports

Approximately ten deacons meetings are scheduled per year for the deacons of Lancaster Baptist Church. They are typically scheduled on a weekday evening at 7:00 PM. A schedule for the year is distributed at the annual Deacons Orientation. (See Appendix 2 for a description of this event.)

While different goals are accomplished at each meeting, a typical agenda for a sample meeting is as follows:

- Open in prayer
- Review widow needs
- Review financial records
- Committee discussions
- Lancaster Baptist School
- West Coast Baptist College

At each meeting, the deacons turn in to the pastor a monthly report. (See sample report in Appendix 7). The purpose of this report is not to "check up" on the deacons, but so the pastor will know that the church members are being cared for on a regular basis. The report includes information on new members contacted, meals delivered, visits made, cards sent, fellowship initiated, and other services performed. These reports are reviewed and filed.

Although the specific needs of each church will be different, the ministries described in this chapter relate to the core duties of church work. I know from experience the immense blessing it is for deacons to come alongside and bear a portion of these responsibilities. Their willing and tireless labor enhances our church's effectiveness for Christ.

CHAPTER SIX

The Relationships of Deacons

In 2006, *Focus on the Family* released these sobering statistics: 1,500 pastors leave the ministry each month due to moral failure, spiritual burnout, or contention in their churches; 70% percent of pastors constantly fight depression and do not have a close friend or confidant; 80% of pastors and 84% of pastors' wives are discouraged with the ministry.

These numbers are staggering, but they are also revealing of the load that a pastor carries as he loves, cares for, and spiritually leads his people. Deacons, however, are placed by God into a unique position in which they can help shoulder some of the pastor's burden.

The relationship between a pastor and a deacon is special. Deacons are not only called to serve the congregation, but also to support and minister to the pastor and his family.

For a man to effectively fulfill his servant-position as a deacon, there are several relationships in which he must be engaged:

Your Relationship with the Lord

No human relationship can reach its spiritual potential without each party developing and maintaining an intimate walk with the Lord. A deacon can only serve his pastor and church family through God's enabling grace, thus he must be regularly at the throne of grace.

Paul expressed the priority he made his own relationship with the Lord when he wrote, *"That I may know him, and the power of his resurrection, and the fellowship of his sufferings, being made conformable unto his death"* (Philippians 3:10).

Like any other relationship, building this one is a continual, daily process: *"As ye have therefore received Christ Jesus the Lord, so **walk ye in him:** Rooted and built up in him, and stablished in the faith, as ye have been taught, abounding therein with thanksgiving"* (Colossians 2:6–7).

A personal, daily walk

A daily quiet time is the single most important factor in developing a relationship with the Lord and living victoriously. Second Chronicles 12:14 tells us that King Rehoboam *"did evil, because he prepared not his heart to seek the LORD."*

To be able to biblically meet the many demands of service to the church family, each deacon must personally study God's Word frequently and thoroughly. *"Study to shew thyself approved unto God, a workman that needeth not to be ashamed, rightly dividing the word of truth"* (2 Timothy 2:15).

Satan targets all Christians, but he seems to aim more of his arrows toward those who are in positions of leadership and service in the church. It is for this reason that deacons must heed the admonition of 1 Timothy 4:16: *"Take heed unto thyself, and unto the doctrine; continue in them: for in doing this thou shalt both save thyself, and them that hear thee."*

A Spirit-filled walk

A key qualification in the selection process of the first seven deacons was that they be *"men…full of the Holy Ghost…"* (Acts 6:3). Only through the power of the Spirit can meaningful, lasting ministry take place. This is why Christ promised his disciples that their power in ministry would come after the Holy Spirit was sent: *"But ye shall receive power, after that the Holy Ghost is come upon you: and ye shall be witnesses unto me both in Jerusalem, and in all Judaea, and in Samaria, and unto the uttermost part of the earth"* (Acts 1:8).

Every Christian is indwelled by the Spirit at the moment of salvation (Ephesians 1:13), but being filled with the Spirit requires daily surrender. A.W. Tozer wrote, "Though every believer has the Holy Spirit, the Holy Spirit does not have every believer." We should follow the example of Andrew Murray who wrote, "I have learned to place myself before God every day as a vessel to be filled with His Holy Spirit."

The story is told of a group of area pastors who were choosing an evangelist for an evangelistic crusade. When one pastor suggested D.L. Moody, a young pastor across the table spoke up. With a bit of jealousy for Moody's success he asked, "Why do we need Moody? He's uneducated and backward. Who does he think he is anyway? Does he think he has a monopoly on the Holy Spirit?" An older, wiser pastor answered, "No, Moody doesn't have a monopoly on the Holy Spirit, but the Holy Spirit has a monopoly on him."

Like Moody, we can only be Spirit-filled as we are willing to surrender to the Holy Spirit's control in our lives. Moody himself said, "I believe firmly that the moment our hearts are emptied of pride and selfishness and ambition and everything that is contrary to God's law, the Holy Spirit will fill every corner of our hearts. But if we are full of pride and conceit and ambition and the world, there is no room for the Spirit of God. We must be emptied before we can be filled."

Only when we give ourselves completely to the Holy Spirit can we have a ministry filled with spiritual fruit. We can do nothing in our strength, but through the power of God, spiritual fruit is abundant. In John 15:5, Christ explained, *"I am the vine, ye are the branches: He that abideth in me, and I in him, the same bringeth forth much fruit: for without me ye can do nothing."*

Corrie ten Boom, a Dutch Christian who is known for her kindness to the Jews during World War II, explained it this way: "Connected with Him in His love, I am more than conqueror; without Him, I am nothing. Like some railway tickets in America, I am not good if detached."

The highest relational priority for a deacon must be his walk with the Lord—daily studying His Word and daily surrendering to His Spirit. As Alexander Maclaren said, "He who has the Holy Spirit in his heart and the Scripture in his hands has all he needs."

Your Relationship with the Lost

Christ expressed His purpose in coming to earth in Luke 19:10, *"For the Son of man is come to seek and to save that which was lost."* Before ascending to Heaven, Christ gave the local church the responsibility of seeking out the lost and telling them of the One who can save them: *"Go ye into all the world, and preach the gospel to every creature"* (Mark 16:15).

The central purpose of the local church is to reach the lost for Christ. Rendering service to church members is important—this is why the office of the deacon was instituted—but service can never substitute for soulwinning. Each Christian must maintain a heart for souls.

At a pastors' training session in Detroit, attendees were given a survey with this question included: "What is your greatest hindrance in witnessing?" The results were revealing. Not one person marked that they didn't really care, but 51% said they were afraid of how the other person would react! Fear of man has silenced many Christians from sharing their faith.

To combat the fear of man, we must focus on what Paul called "the terror of the Lord." Paul had every outward reason to fear man. When people rejected Paul's message of the Gospel, they beat, stoned, or imprisoned him! Yet, Paul wrote, *"Knowing therefore the terror of the Lord, we persuade men…"* (2 Corinthians 5:11).

Every believer can share his faith. Soulwinning has been simply described as "one beggar telling another beggar where he found bread." Anyone can do that!

After a service in which D.L. Moody preached, a woman expressed her dislike for his method of evangelism. "I don't really like mine all that much either," Moody replied, "What's yours?" After a brief pause, she said, "I don't have one." Moody answered, "Then I prefer my way of doing it to your way of not doing it."

How should a deacon be a wise steward of his relationship with the lost?

Always maintain your testimony.

Remember people are always watching you. A classic example of this truth is personified in Stephen—one of the first deacons. When he was martyred for preaching the Gospel, a man named Saul witnessed Stephen's testimony—a testimony so pure and strong that it made a difference in Saul's life. Saul, later called Paul, was eventually saved and became a missionary, taking the Gospel throughout the known world.

Peter emphasized the importance of a godly testimony and lifestyle in reaching the lost:

> *Having your conversation honest among the Gentiles: that, whereas they speak against you as evildoers, they may by your good works, which they shall behold, glorify God in the day of visitation.*—1 PETER 2:12

But sanctify the Lord God in your hearts: and be ready always to give an answer to every man that asketh you a reason of the hope that is in you with meekness and fear: Having a good conscience; that, whereas they speak evil of you, as of evildoers, they may be ashamed that falsely accuse your good conversation in Christ.—1 PETER 3:15–16

A godly testimony makes an impact. One report explained, "Christianity is not losing influence in America because it is overmatched by challenges of the day; it is losing its impact because believers have been unsuccessful at merging faith and lifestyle outside the walls of the church."[1] Every deacon should ask himself, "Does my lifestyle throughout the week strengthen or weaken my witness for Christ?"

We are commissioned as Christ's representatives on the earth. Second Corinthians 5:20 says, *"Now then we are ambassadors for Christ, as though God did beseech you by us: we pray you in Christ's stead, be ye reconciled to God."* We must wisely steward our testimonies so that others will be drawn to Christ.

Always remember everyone has an eternal destiny.

Every person with whom you come in contact will spend eternity in Heaven or Hell. Hebrews 9:27 reminds us of this sobering truth, *"And as it is appointed unto men once to die, but after this the judgment."* Living in the reality of this truth helps overcome the fear of man in witnessing; it turns our attention from a lost person's possible rejection of our message to the greatness of his need.

For us who have trusted Christ as Saviour, spending eternity with Christ is one of our greatest anticipations, and we look forward to His return. Should we not, then, do all we can until that time to tell others of the saving grace of God? Oswald J. Smith once said,

---

1   From the Barna Report, November/December 1997 (Word Ministry Resources), quoted in The Promise Keeper, January, 1999, p. 6

"We talk of the Second Coming when half of the world has never even heard of the first."

C.T. Studd was a missionary to cannibal tribes in Africa for many years. Because he was physically weak and often plagued with jungle fevers, loving friends encouraged Studd to stay in his home country. But with a greater love for the souls of others than for his own comfort, he said, "Some wish to live within the sound of a chapel bell; I wish to run a rescue mission within a yard of Hell."

The purpose of the local church is to reach the lost, and every deacon should be actively involved in reaching others with the Gospel.

Your Relationship with the Pastor

The pastor-deacon relationship is key to the health and growth of the church. Here are some keys to help you nurture this relationship:

The pastor is your friend.

The pastor has literally chosen to give his life to the church. Paul told the Corinthian church, "*I will very gladly spend and be spent for you; though the more abundantly I love you, the less I be loved*" (2 Corinthians 12:15). Even when Paul's love was not returned and his sacrifice was unappreciated, he *wanted* to give of himself for this church. This is the heart of a spiritual shepherd.

The willingness with which a pastor invests himself into his church reflects the greatness of his love. Jesus said, "*This is my commandment, That ye love one another, as I have loved you. Greater love hath no man than this, that a man lay down his life for his friends*" (John 15:12–13).

The pastor's heart is to give in every way he can to the deacons. He wants to serve each of them and their families. Pastors should reiterate to their deacons the words of Paul, "*For ye are our glory and joy*" (1 Thessalonians 2:20).

One pastor wrote, "I love to view all my Christian friends as fuel. Having gathered you all together at my hearth, I warm myself at your fire, and find my Christian love burns and glows." This statement should describe every pastor-deacon friendship.

The pastor appoints various tasks.

The first deacons were called to lighten the administrative load of the apostles. In this case, they were appointed to care for the daily needs of widows in the church.

A deacon's goal should be to help lighten the load of the pastor. D.L. Moody said it like this, "I'd rather put ten men to work than do the work of ten men." Have a willing and a ready spirit to put whole-hearted effort into whatever tasks the pastor assigns. Hebrews 13:17 admonishes, *"Obey them that have the rule over you, and submit yourselves: for they watch for your souls, as they that must give account, that they may do it with joy, and not with grief: for that is unprofitable for you."*

Your relationship with the pastor should ultimately strengthen his relationship with the Lord and the congregation.

The pastor's responsibility to the congregation is tremendous. Hebrews 13:7 and 18 exhort the church to remember and follow their pastor and to pray for him: *"Remember them which have the rule over you, who have spoken unto you the word of God: whose faith follow, considering the end of their conversation. Pray for us: for we trust we have a good conscience, in all things willing to live honestly."*

As a spiritual shepherd, the pastor cares for the flock that God has entrusted to His care. He is commanded to feed the flock and oversee them with servant leadership:

> *Take heed therefore unto yourselves, and to all the flock, over the which the Holy Ghost hath made you overseers, to feed*

the church of God, which he hath purchased with his own blood—ACTS 20:28

The elders which are among you I exhort, who am also an elder, and a witness of the sufferings of Christ, and also a partaker of the glory that shall be revealed: Feed the flock of God which is among you, taking the oversight thereof, not by constraint, but willingly; not for filthy lucre, but of a ready mind; Neither as being lords over God's heritage, but being ensamples to the flock—1 PETER 5:1–3

To feed the flock, the pastor must maintain a growing relationship with the Lord himself. A deacon can help the pastor in this by encouraging him in the Lord and by being willing to assume whatever tasks the pastor can give to free the pastor's time for study. Deacons can also express the pastor's love and care to church members as they serve them, such as the first deacons must have done as they cared for the widows.

Your Relationship with the Staff

The church staff serves as an extension of the pastor's ministry. Thus, as deacons serve the staff, they are in actuality serving their pastor and helping to increase his ministry.

The staff reports to the pastor.

The pastor chooses his staff based on what he discerns the church needs to grow, and he assigns duties to the staff based on each persons abilities and spiritual gifts. The staff then reports directly to the pastor in relation to their responsibilities and ministry.

The staff does not always know what the pastor shares with the deacons. This would especially be true concerning sensitive information that does not directly involve the staff. The deacons should love and encourage the staff—just as they do for all other church members.

The pastor should remember the staff.

As the staff gives of themselves to support and extend the pastor, he should remember them financially at special times, such as Christmas, birthdays, significant employment anniversaries, etc. Scripture often speaks of rewarding those who serve.

> *Withhold not good from them to whom it is due, when it is in the power of thine hand to do it.*—PROVERBS 3:27

> *I have shewed you all things, how that so labouring ye ought to support the weak, and to remember the words of the Lord Jesus, how he said, It is more blessed to give than to receive.* —ACTS 20:35

> *Render therefore to all their dues: tribute to whom tribute is due; custom to whom custom; fear to whom fear; honour to whom honour.*—ROMANS 13:7

Your Relationship with the Finance Department

Church finances should be handled with the highest levels of accountability and faithfulness. First Corinthians 4:2 says, "*Moreover it is required in stewards, that a man be found faithful.*"

How grievous it must be to the Lord when His name is brought low through the financial scandals of churches! Even just one fraudulent report is quickly spread and becomes widely known.

To avoid even a hint of dishonesty, the church should have a strictly followed process for financial reports. At Lancaster Baptist Church, the financial administrator reports to the pastor regularly.

The pastor then shares these reports at the monthly meetings with the deacons. Special accounting questions are addressed to the pastor.

If the financial administrator had to report to all the deacons, he would feel like he had many bosses. At Lancaster Baptist Church, we appoint a rotating finance committee from within the deacons who also confers with the Finance Director. This committee reviews financial statements, the accountable reimbursement program of the church, and other matters. The pastor is always made aware of these meetings in writing. He may attend any such meetings if his schedule permits.

Your Relationship with the Church Family

Deacons should purposefully develop godly relationships with church members to encourage them in their spiritual growth.

Serve them.

The word *deacon* in the New Testament is translated from the Greek word *diakonos,* which simply means "a servant." This is the primary responsibility of deacons—to serve.

Galatians 5:13 says, *"For, brethren, ye have been called unto liberty; only use not liberty for an occasion to the flesh, but by **love serve one another**"* (emphasis mine).

Too often, we want good service, but we don't want to be good servants. Serving, however, is the privilege of mature Christians. We have the opportunity to set our own comfort aside to encourage spiritual growth in others. Romans 15:1–2 says, *"We then that are strong ought to bear the infirmities of the weak, and not to please ourselves. Let every one of us please his neighbour for his good to edification."*

Set an example for them.

Even as Jesus washed the feet of His disciples, deacons should model loving Christian service to the church family.

> *So after he had washed their feet, and had taken his garments, and was set down again, he said unto them, Know ye what I have done to you? Ye call me Master and Lord: and ye say well; for so I am. If I then, your Lord and Master, have washed your feet; ye also ought to wash one another's feet. For I have given you an example, that ye should do as I have done to you. Verily, verily, I say unto you, The servant is not greater than his lord; neither he that is sent greater than he that sent him. If ye know these things, happy are ye if ye do them.*
> —John 13:12–17

Forgive them.

Those who serve others will inevitably be taken for granted, misunderstood, taken advantage of, and slandered. Deacons should choose, even before being wounded, that they will forgive.

Forgiveness is possible, even for the greatest of offences, when we remember the greatness of God's forgiveness toward us. Our sin against Him is far greater than any human could commit against us; yet He willingly forgave us. Thus Colossians 3:13 instructs us, "*Forbearing one another, and forgiving one another, if any man have a quarrel against any: even as Christ forgave you, so also do ye.*"

As someone once said, "We base our forgiveness on what God has done for us, not on what another person has done to us." It is the grace of God within us that gives us the power to forgive. "*And be ye kind one to another, tenderhearted, forgiving one another, even as God for Christ's sake hath forgiven you*" (Ephesians 4:32).

The goal of forgiveness is that the offending brother would repent and be restored in his relationship with the Lord and his church family. Galatians 6:1 points out that it is the spiritually mature Christian who is responsible to initiate the process of restoration: "*Brethren, if a man be overtaken in a fault, ye which are spiritual, restore such an one in the spirit of meekness; considering thyself, lest thou also be tempted.*"

Involve them.

Each Christian has been especially equipped by God with spiritual gifts to serve Him in the local church.

> *And he gave some, apostles; and some, prophets; and some, evangelists; and some, pastors and teachers; For the perfecting of the saints, for the work of the ministry, for the edifying of the body of Christ: Till we all come in the unity of the faith, and of the knowledge of the Son of God, unto a perfect man, unto the measure of the stature of the fulness of Christ: That we henceforth be no more children, tossed to and fro, and carried about with every wind of doctrine, by the sleight of men, and cunning craftiness, whereby they lie in wait to deceive*—EPHESIANS 4:11–14

Deacons can help church members reach their potential of joyful Christian service by including them in local church ministry. Deacons should encourage church members to be involved in the church by inviting members to serve along side them.

Be humble with them.

Winston Churchill was once asked, "Doesn't it thrill you to know that every time you make a speech, the hall is packed to overflowing?" "It's quite flattering," he replied, "but whenever I feel that way, I always remember that if instead of making a political speech I was being hanged, the crowd would be twice as big."

If pride is evident in a deacon's life, he forgets his purpose of serving and neglects caring for the most basic and needful duties of service. Romans 12:15 says, *"Rejoice with them that do rejoice, and weep with them that weep."* This reminds us that service is others-focused. And it only requires a heart humble enough to think of others first. Church members should always know that the deacons are available to serve in as simple a way as rejoicing with or sorrowing with another as needed.

God promises to give grace to the humble and to exalt them in due time.

> *But he giveth more grace. Wherefore he saith, God resisteth the proud, but giveth grace unto the humble.* —James 4:6

> *Whosoever therefore shall humble himself as this little child, the same is greatest in the kingdom of heaven.* —Matthew 18:4

> *And whosoever shall exalt himself shall be abased; and he that shall humble himself shall be exalted.* —Matthew 23:12

> *Humble yourselves therefore under the mighty hand of God, that he may exalt you in due time:*—1 Peter 5:6

To the church family, the word *deacon* should simply be a synonym for *servant*.

Don't discuss deacons meetings.

Often confidential information is shared or discussed in these meetings. Sharing information that others don't need to know would damage the church family.

Proverbs describes the deacon who serves his church family through wisdom with his words:

> *A prudent man concealeth knowledge: but the heart of fools proclaimeth foolishness.*—Proverbs 12:23

A talebearer revealeth secrets: but he that is of a faithful spirit concealeth the matter.—Proverbs 11:13

Work at getting to know new members.

The larger a church grows, the greater of a challenge this becomes. Yet to appropriately *serve* the church, deacons must *know* the church. As new people join, reach out to and befriend them. Proverbs 18:24 says, *"A man that hath friends must shew himself friendly: and there is a friend that sticketh closer than a brother."*

Your Relationship with One Another

Among the circle of deacons, there must be a bond of unity and fellowship to serve together in accomplishing the work of God.

Pray for one another.

Prayer knits Christian hearts together, and prayer is one of the greatest needs for ministry. Even the Apostle Paul sensed this need and specifically asked his churches to pray for him.

> *Praying always with all prayer and supplication in the Spirit, and watching thereunto with all perseverance and supplication for all saints; And for me, that utterance may be given unto me, that I may open my mouth boldly, to make known the mystery of the gospel,*—Ephesians 6:18–19

> *Finally, brethren, pray for us, that the word of the Lord may have free course, and be glorified, even as it is with you:*—2 Thessalonians 3:1

James 5:16 promises, *"The effectual fervent prayer of a righteous man availeth much."*

Be a team with one another.

One of the most frustrating things to watch is a sports team in which one individual wants to be the star—even at the expense of the team's success. The famed football coach Vince Lombardi said, "The only true satisfaction a player receives is the satisfaction that comes from being part of a successful team, regardless of his personal accomplishments."

The church is a team, and each person must yield his personal rights for the success of others and the cause of Christ.

> If there be therefore any consolation in Christ, if any comfort of love, if any fellowship of the Spirit, if any bowels and mercies, Fulfil ye my joy, that ye be likeminded, having the same love, being of one accord, of one mind. Let nothing be done through strife or vainglory; but in lowliness of mind let each esteem other better than themselves. Look not every man on his own things, but every man also on the things of others.—PHILIPPIANS 2:1–4

John Wooden was the first man to ever be inducted into the basketball Hall of Fame as both a player and a coach. He led Purdue University to the national championship in 1932. Then he became a successful basketball coach in Indiana before taking over the head job at UCLA. There, Coach John Wooden won ten national championships, a record that may never be broken. Wooden attributed his success, in part, to the unselfishness of his players. He said, "Generally speaking, individual performances don't win games. Teamwork wins games."

Teamwork makes serving together enjoyable. First Thessalonians 5:11 tells us, "Wherefore comfort yourselves together, and edify one another, even as also ye do."

Appreciate one another.

Everyone has different spiritual gifts.

For I say, through the grace given unto me, to every man that is among you, not to think of himself more highly than he ought to think; but to think soberly, according as God hath dealt to every man the measure of faith. For as we have many members in one body, and all members have not the same office: So we, being many, are one body in Christ, and every one members one of another. Having then gifts differing according to the grace that is given to us, whether prophecy, let us prophesy according to the proportion of faith; Or ministry, let us wait on our ministering: or he that teacheth, on teaching; Or he that exhorteth, on exhortation: he that giveth, let him do it with simplicity; he that ruleth, with diligence; he that sheweth mercy, with cheerfulness.—ROMANS 12:3–8

Often those with different spiritual gifts will approach a matter differently. This can cause friction, unless both people learn to appreciate the larger perspective gained through multiple spiritual gifts.

Communicate with one another.

Paul was a communicator. Often in his epistles, he would conclude with personal communication—greetings, recommendations, information about his personal well being. As he closed Ephesians, he recognized that the church needed to hear how he was doing in prison, so he sent Tychicus to communicate in his place.

For which I am an ambassador in bonds: that therein I may speak boldly, as I ought to speak. But that ye also may know my affairs, and how I do, Tychicus, a beloved brother and faithful minister in the Lord, shall make known to you all things: Whom I have sent unto you for the same purpose, that ye might know

our affairs, and that he might comfort your hearts.
—EPHESIANS 6:20–22

Maintain clear and open communication with fellow deacons. Most interpersonal tensions are caused by a lack of communication, and they are solved—or even better, prevented— by clear communication.

Your Relationship with Your Wife

An eighty-five-year-old man was out fishing one day when he heard someone say, "Pick me up." Surprised because he had no one with him, he looked around. He didn't see anyone, but he heard the voice again, "Pick me up." He just about concluded he must be dreaming when he looked down and saw a frog.

In amazement, the man said, "Are you talking to me?"

"Yes," the frog answered. "Pick me up, and kiss me. I will turn into a beautiful bride."

The man picked up the frog and put her in his pocket.

"Wait," called out the frog. "Aren't you going to kiss me?"

"No thanks," the man answered. "At my age, I'd rather have a talking frog."

Wise is the man who appreciates his godly wife! Proverbs 31:10 says, *"Who can find a virtuous woman? for her price is far above rubies."* How can you demonstrate your love and gratefulness to your bride?

Love her.

Ephesians 5:25 instructs husbands to love their wives with the unselfish and unconditional love Christ gives the church: *"Husbands, love your wives, even as Christ also loved the church, and gave himself for it."*

Satan continually works to divide a husband and wife with bitterness. This is why Colossians 3:19 specifically instructs, *"Husbands, love your wives, and be not bitter against them."*

Be sensitive to her.

God has designed ladies with more sensitive emotions than men. First Peter 3:7 teaches husbands to honor and be sensitive toward their wives' emotions: *"Likewise, ye husbands, dwell with them according to knowledge, giving honour unto the wife, as unto the weaker vessel, and as being heirs together of the grace of life; that your prayers be not hindered."*

Lead her.

Marriage was designed by God with unique roles for the husband and the wife. The husband's role is to spiritually lead his wife: *"For the husband is the head of the wife, even as Christ is the head of the church: and he is the saviour of the body"* (Ephesians 5:23).

When Paul gave Timothy the qualifications for deacons, he specifically mentioned that the deacon must lead his home:

> *Likewise must the deacons be grave, not doubletongued, not given to much wine, not greedy of filthy lucre; Holding the mystery of the faith in a pure conscience. And let these also first be proved; then let them use the office of a deacon, being found blameless. Even so must their wives be grave, not slanderers, sober, faithful in all things. Let the deacons be the husbands of one wife, ruling their children and their own houses well. For they that have used the office of a deacon well purchase to themselves a good degree, and great boldness in the faith which is in Christ Jesus.*—1 TIMOTHY 3:8–13

Communicate with her.

Marriages *need* communication to flourish, and wives often sense this need more acutely than their husbands.

When God joins a man and a woman in a "one flesh" union, what concerns one should concern the other. They must communicate with each other.

> *So ought men to love their wives as their own bodies.*
> *He that loveth his wife loveth himself. For no man ever*
> *yet hated his own flesh; but nourisheth and cherisheth*
> *it, even as the Lord the church: For we are members of*
> *his body, of his flesh, and of his bones. For this cause*
> *shall a man leave his father and mother, and shall*
> *be joined unto his wife, and they two shall be one*
> *flesh.*—EPHESIANS 5:28–31

Deacons' wives should not be expected to bear the same burden in ministry as their husbands; they are not "deaconesses." A deacon's wife is simply that—the wife of the deacon. Her ministry is one of helps—to support and complete her husband.

Each of the many relationships of the deacon requires care and prayer. As a deacon invests himself in building these relationships, he will increase his effectiveness and enlarge his capacity for ministry.

CHAPTER SEVEN

The Deacon's Wife

Many biographies of spiritual leaders, men whom God has used greatly to serve His people, have a common denominator—a loyal, godly wife who is an encourager to her husband. Adoniram Judson, Hudson Taylor, William Booth, George Muller, Jonathan Goforth, and John Bunyan all knew the blessing of having their ministry multiplied and their influence extended through their wives.

Truly, a woman's part in her husband's ministry is powerful. Her support can uplift him and increase his ministry, or her indifference or negativity can diminish his effectiveness.

The wives of the men listed above all served alongside their husbands in different capacities. Some ministered more visibly than others, helping in public ministry. Yet, in every case, in whatever role, the greatest assistance these wives offered was their ministry directly to their husbands. They were first the completers and fulfillers of their husbands, and then they offered support in his work.

The deacon's wife has a unique and vital role in the ministry of her husband, and thus in the ministry of her entire church. As mentioned earlier, she is not a "deaconess," bearing the same ministry description as that of her husband. She is a deacon's wife, and her primary ministry is to be her husband's completer. Part of her ministry to her husband will undoubtedly include serving with him as he serves the church.

The Joy in Serving

At our annual Deacons Orientation several years ago, my wife prepared a session for our deacons' wives to encourage them to maintain a joyful spirit in their ministry. First at home and then in the church, she encouraged them to find joy in serving. This chapter is taken from her notes:

Serving our husbands and our church family is an opportunity to be treasured. Sometimes, however, our heart to serve grows cold, and our service eventually suffers.

In the book of Philippians, Paul majors on joy. These four short chapters point out truths that can keep our joy cup overflowing as we serve.

Labor for the Lord.

When we serve for man's approval, our joy will fluctuate with their level of appreciation. Yet when we minister to others *"as to the Lord, and not unto men,"* we can always rejoice, *"Knowing that of the Lord ye shall receive the reward of the inheritance: for ye serve the Lord Christ"* (Colossians 3:23–24).

Although Paul dearly loved the church at Philippi, his chief goal was that *"Christ shall be magnified in my body"* (Philippians 1:20). We must keep the Lord the object of worship as we serve others.

Lavish encouragement.

Keep looking for the good. Your husband needs you to be his cheerleader. Your church family needs you to encourage spiritual growth by praising their progress along the way.

The book of Philippians is full of Paul's encouragement to the church at Philippi. What a motivation it must have been for them to read: *"I thank my God upon every remembrance of you, Always in every prayer of mine for you all making request with joy... For God is my record, how greatly I long after you all in the bowels of Jesus Christ. ...Therefore, my brethren dearly beloved and longed for, my joy and crown, so stand fast in the Lord, my dearly beloved"* (Philippians 1:3–4, 8; 4:1). He freely told this church of his love for them and his joy in their spiritual progress.

Look for God's hand in everything.

Amazingly, Paul wrote this epistle of joy from a Roman prison. No doubt in great physical discomfort, Paul rejoiced in God's greater purposes and he traced God's work through his suffering. In Philippians 1:12 he explained, *"But I would ye should understand, brethren, that the things which happened unto me have fallen out rather unto the furtherance of the gospel"* (Philippians 1:12). Even in the midst of pressures and burdens, look for God's hand of grace, and rejoice in His promise to work all things for good for those who love Him (Romans 8:28).

Live expectantly.

Too easily we slip into autopilot, a mode where we routinely fulfill our duties, but we labor without the joy of anticipating God's blessing. God has assured us that He will reward every act of service offered with a pure motive for Him (1 Corinthians 3:11–14), and He desires that we serve expectantly.

Even as Paul faced execution, he did so with the expectancy of eternal rewards for his ministry investments: *"According to my earnest expectation and my hope, that in nothing I shall be ashamed, but that with all boldness, as always, so now also Christ shall be magnified in my body, whether it be by life, or by death"* (Philippians 1:20).

Let the past go.

Because we live in a world of imperfect people (and we each contribute to that imperfection ourselves!) we will be hurt. And if you love and serve others, you increase your liability for being wounded. Paul's first trip to Philippi included a beating and a night in prison (Acts 16:19–40), yet the book of Philippians doesn't even mention this experience. Rather, Paul majors on the ministry of the present.

Just as we cannot drive staring in the rearview mirror, so we cannot effectively minister while constantly rehearsing the wounds of our past. Philippians 3:13–14 says, *"Brethren, I count not myself to have apprehended: but this one thing I do, forgetting those things which are behind, and reaching forth unto those things which are before, I press toward the mark for the prize of the high calling of God in Christ Jesus."* Let the past be behind you by forgiving others, and press forward as you continue serving.

Learn to be thankful.

A grateful spirit enhances joy exponentially! It turns our minds from the problems and focuses our hearts on the blessings. Philippians 4:6 tells us to give thanks even as we bring our difficult requests to the Lord: *Be careful for nothing; but in every thing by prayer and supplication with thanksgiving let your requests be made known unto God."*

An attitude of gratefulness is a learned trait, perfected by practice. Learn to offer the Lord the continual *"sacrifice of praise"* (Hebrews 13:15) regardless of how you feel, for He is always worthy. Look for ways to express thankfulness to others as well. It will encourage both you and others around.

Linger on the positive.

The root of unhappiness is found in our thoughts. Pessimistic thoughts can cloud the sunniest of days, while thoughts filled with thanksgiving and rejoicing can brighten the darkest nights. Philippians 4:8 provides a checklist for the thoughts we should allow to linger in our minds: *"Finally, brethren, whatsoever things are true, whatsoever things are honest, whatsoever things are just, whatsoever things are pure, whatsoever things are lovely, whatsoever things are of good report; if there be any virtue, and if there be any praise, think on these things."*

Lean on God's power.

If you think the ministry of a deacon's wife is too much for you, you're right! When we attempt to minister to others, even our husbands and children, in our own strength, we will soon discover our insufficiency. God used Paul to accomplish much, but it was all done "through Christ." Philippians 4:13 says, *"I can do all things through Christ which strengtheneth me."*

Paul's greatest joy in ministry was not in what he accomplished, and his greatest goal was not in accomplishing more. His joy was found in knowing Christ, and he rejoiced in any experience that brought him closer to Christ. In Philippians 3:10 he expressed his great ambition to know Christ intimately: *"That I may know him, and the power of his resurrection, and the fellowship of his sufferings, being made conformable unto his death."*

Although the book of Philippians carries the theme of joy, it is centered around Christ. When Christ is the center of our lives and the focus of our service, joy will be the inevitable by-product.

The Testimony of a Deacon's Wife

The influence of a deacon's wife in the church is so great that God required similar qualifications for her as for the deacon himself:

"Even so must their wives be grave, not slanderers, sober, faithful in all things" (1 Timothy 3:11).

This list is similar to the first several qualifications for deacons (chapter 3). Let's examine them briefly as specifically applied to wives:

Grave—Every deacon's wife should be filled with the joy of the Lord, and that joy should be evident in her countenance. Yet, she must also place importance on spiritual matters and take her husband's and her own leadership responsibilities seriously. She should manage her schedule so as to make room for ministry to others.

Not slanderers—The power of the tongue is greater than we can fathom. Proverbs 18:21 says, *"Death and life are in the power of the tongue: and they that love it shall eat the fruit thereof."* Gossip, slander, and backbiting have destroyed many churches as hurtful words tear down leadership and create deep rifts in fellowship. Deacons' wives must set the standard in avoiding these kinds of communication. When offered a sampling of slander, they should be quick to encourage wholesome, edifying words instead.

Occasionally, deacons' wives may become aware of confidential information. In these cases, they must be very careful to hold confidentiality and protect those involved from critique or criticism.

Sober—Related to the deacon's qualification *"not given to much wine,"* this indicates a woman who is temperate and free from excess in any area. Her life is disciplined and brought under the control of the Holy Spirit.

Faithful in all things—A deacon's wife should be a model of faithfulness in every area—to the Lord, her husband, her family, and her church.

In your walk with the Lord, be consistent, spending time in His Word daily. To disciple others in Christian growth, you will need a maintained and vibrant walk with the Lord in your own life. Daily pray for your husband, children, pastor, church family, and for other deacons' wives.

As a wife and mother, make your marriage and your family a priority. Remember, your primary responsibility as a deacon's wife is to complete your husband.

One of the greatest ways you can serve your church is by being faithful to all services. You should regularly and visibly attend with your family. Other ladies in the church notice when you are absent, and this obvious lack of commitment discourages faithfulness in their lives as well. Come early to greet and encourage others, and stay a few minutes after church to do the same.

Attend a weekly soulwinning rally, and be faithful in door-knocking and visitation. Be present at all scheduled church activities including special meetings, ladies events, deacons' wives fellowships, and Sunday school activities. Express a willingness to go the extra mile by offering to help in setup and cleanup for ladies activities and by being available for extra nursery help when needed.

Be an encourager to your pastor's wife by praying for her regularly and writing her encouraging notes. My wife, Terrie, has often been blessed and encouraged by our deacons' wives and their love and care for her.

"Faithful in all things" is the mark of a spiritually mature Christian who strives for balance and consistency in her life. And it describes a woman who places importance on her commitments to the Lord and others.

These requirements for deacons' wives are significant. A wife's deficiency in these areas would literally disqualify her husband from holding the office of a deacon. Although no woman is perfect, the description of 1 Timothy 3:11 should be characteristic of a deacon's wife: "...grave, not slanderers, sober, faithful in all things."

The Responsibilities of a Deacon's Wife

The role a deacon's wife fulfills is a vital, biblical role. At Lancaster Baptist Church, there are several areas of service that are uniquely performed by the deacons and their wives. These roles are not given to the general congregation or the staff, but to the deacons and their wives.

Altar work

Our deacons' wives are ready and alert to help with altar work during the invitation of every service, unless they are in another ministry during that service time. (See chapter 9 for helps for altar work.)

New members' reception

A reception for the new members of the church is held once a quarter after the evening service. This allows and encourages the church family to introduce themselves to the new members and enjoy a cake reception and time of fellowship. The deacons and their wives help prepare for and host these receptions.

Lord's Table

The deacons serve the Lord's Table, and each deacon's wife is placed into a group that, on a rotating basis, helps with setup or cleanup for the Lord's Table. This is a sacred time for the church family and should be treated with the right spirit. Deacons' wives should take care that their heart is prepared and ready, not only when partaking of the Lord's Table, but also during its setup.

The Care and Ministry of a Deacon's Wife

In addition to the responsibilities above, our deacons and their wives provide the following care and service to our church family:

Undershepherd ministry

Every member of our church is on an undershepherd list which is divided and assigned to the deacons annually. Deacon couples should get to know the people on their lists and provide encouragement for them. Ways to do this include writing notes; recognizing birthdays, anniversaries, and special days; encouraging attendance to church events; and supporting those going through trials.

Many members of our church also have a care group leader (assigned through the adult Bible classes). There are, however, some members who are not enrolled in adult Bible classes, and thus the deacon couple are their only assigned "care givers." In these cases, deacons and their wives also provide the care normally given by the care group leader by arranging for the home delivery of meals after births and hospitalizations.

Widows and shut-ins

Elderly widows, widowers, and shut-ins are assigned to each deacon couple. Together, deacon couples can provide special care, which might include household repairs, rides to and from the doctor, rides to church, etc. As a deacon's wife, you should accompany your husband when he visits a widow or any ladies in the church.

Funerals

Although the pastoral staff and adult Bible class teachers minister to families during times of loss, the deacons and their wives are also asked to pray for, visit, and care for the family as well as attending the funeral if possible. They arrange home-delivered meals for the family following the death, and they coordinate the family reception after the funeral.

The deacon's wife is the helper of her husband, and her ministry to him directly affects his ministry to the church. Sometimes her service is behind the scenes as she encourages and loves her husband, and sometimes in hands-on service to others. Either way, her role is vital and her care needful in the local church.

PART TWO

Practical Helps for Deacons

CHAPTER EIGHT

Biblically Handling Criticism

American author Elbert Hubbord wrote, "To avoid criticism, do nothing, say nothing, be nothing." Unfortunately, a deacon's very job description requires that he do, say, and be—do for others, speak for the Lord, and be a godly Christian. Thus, he can count on encountering criticism.

The question then is not how to *avoid* criticism, but how to *respond* to it. You cannot control in which direction others' shoot their darts of criticism, but you can control your response. Following are several pointers on biblically handling criticism.

Consider the Accuracy of the Criticism

Some criticism really does reflect, or at least partially reflect, the truth. Before disregarding all negative remarks about you or your ministry, bring them before the Lord. Ask Him to search your heart and reveal any areas of needed growth the criticism may expose.

With true humility and deep confidence in God's love, David exposed his heart for the Lord's inspection when he prayed, *"Search me, O God, and know my heart: try me, and know my thoughts: And see if there be any wicked way in me, and lead me in the way everlasting"* (Psalm 139:23–24).

Never be afraid to bring criticism before the Lord for evaluation. If the critic was wrong in his appraisal, nothing is lost; if he was right, God can use him to change you.

Leave It with the Lord

There is no need to continually rehash hurtful comments in your own mind. Once you bring it to the Lord and ask Him to search your heart and motives, *leave it with Him.* First Peter 5:7 encourages, *"Casting all your care upon him; for he careth for you."*

Don't Develop a Persecution Complex

Criticism comes to everyone who invests their life in others. First Peter 4:12–13 says, *"Beloved, think it not strange concerning the fiery trial which is to try you, as though some strange thing happened unto you: But rejoice, inasmuch as ye are partakers of Christ's sufferings; that, when his glory shall be revealed, ye may be glad also with exceeding joy."*

Don't allow Satan to use the voice of a critic to blind you to the many people who are behind you, who love and support you. Even if the criticism is true, there are many (including your pastor) who love you unconditionally and who haven't allowed criticism to change their heart for you.

Don't Seek Retaliation

Never attempt to get even with your critics; the Lord will take care of it in His time. Romans 12:19 admonishes, *"Dearly beloved, avenge not yourselves, but rather give place unto wrath: for it is written, Vengeance is mine; I will repay, saith the Lord."* When we attempt to take vengeance into our own hands, we demonstrate that we mistrust the sovereignty of our God.

Jesus points us to a better response than retaliation—prayer. Luke 6:27–28 says, *"But I say unto you which hear, Love your enemies, do good to them which hate you, Bless them that curse you, and pray for them which despitefully use you."* A common Christian cliché notes that "prayer changes things"; however, prayer changes people as well. Sincerely ask the Lord to change the heart and mind of your critic.

Remember, too, that regardless of what your prayers do for your critic, they will change *you.* Praying for others, even those who have hurt you, increases your love for them, and it opens your heart to God's Spirit to minister grace to you.

Seek Reconciliation When Possible

You may need to go to your critic and endeavor to gain a brother. Matthew 18:15 says, *"Moreover if thy brother shall trespass against thee, go and tell him his fault between thee and him alone: if he shall hear thee, thou hast gained thy brother."* Be sure that you approach him in a spirit of humility and love.

Refuse to Be a Sounding Board for Criticism

Not all criticism in the church will be leveled *at* you; some people will attempt to criticize *with you.* When people attempt to bring their dissatisfaction regarding church matters, the pastor, or other church members to you, refuse to be their sounding board.

Sometimes you can offer to pray with the person regarding that which is troubling them. Criticism is really an expression of pride in one's ability to accurately appraise the shortcomings of others; but prayer requires humility as we ask God to work the change which we cannot effect. Critics usually would rather continue their slander than humble themselves in prayer, thus offering to pray about the matter will often discourage a critic from bringing future criticism your way.

Regardless of your specific response, choose the path of loyalty. Joining with a critic will only hurt the church and wound others. Your job is to serve the church, building by edification. We must each heed the instruction of Ephesians 4:29: *"Let no corrupt communication proceed out of your mouth, but that which is good to the use of edifying, that it may minister grace unto the hearers."*

When the criticism brought to you is over minor issues, shield the pastor from hearing it if possible. Hearing every small complaint in the church would tend to discourage the pastor. If, however, a trend of criticism is developing over minor issues or you know a major criticism is developing, it is important to inform the pastor.

Seek Help When Needed

If you become discouraged over a problem in the church, don't allow your discouragement to be viewed by other church members. This will simply encourage criticism and complaints. Instead, set up a meeting with the pastor to explain your concern.

Hebrews 13:17 describes pastors as men who *"watch for your souls."* Allow your pastor to shepherd you through any legitimate problems that have become a concern to you. If you need your pastor's help, don't allow the problem to fester in your heart. This only makes you more vulnerable to sharing your discouragement with a critic, and the delay will make it more difficult for you to receive the help of your pastor.

Maintain an Accurate Perspective

Criticism comes whether or not you are doing a good job. This truth is illustrated by two taxidermists who stopped along the street in front of an owl on display. Together, they criticized the taxidermy job represented. They said that its feathers were rumpled, its eyes looked too glassy, its feet weren't positioned properly, and its wings were out of proportion. They were surprised a moment later when the owl flew away.

Although these men felt they were experts in their field, they were simply mistaken. Don't allow the criticism of self-proclaimed experts who misunderstand your motives or misinterpret your service to discourage you. Simply "fly away," faithfully continuing to serve others.

Remain Faithful

One of the most subtle dangers of criticism is its ability to distract those it attacks from the real battle. Ephesians 6:12 pulls back the curtain to reveal the true nature of our struggles: *"For we wrestle not against flesh and blood, but against principalities, against powers, against the rulers of the darkness of this world, against spiritual wickedness in high places."*

We are engaged in a spiritual battle, not a fleshly one. The mission Christ has given the church is to declare the Gospel to the entire world and to disciple those who trust Christ as their Saviour. To allow criticism to distract us from our true mission only hinders the work of God.

In the larger picture, criticism regarding people is trivial and petty. We must keep insignificant issues in perspective and remain faithful in the main work of winning souls for Christ.

CHAPTER NINE

Altar Counseling

One of the primary ministries of the deacons at Lancaster Baptist Church is doing the work of counseling after each message is preached. At the Deacons Orientation (see Appendix 2), training is often given to the deacons and their wives, showing them how to lead someone to Christ, how to explain baptism, or how to receive new members into the church.

Deacons and their wives should be ready and alert to help with altar work at every service, unless serving in another ministry at that time. They are to come forward during the invitation prayer and watch the pastoral staff for needs. Deacons should assist men at the altar, and deacons' wives should assist ladies.

Leading Someone to Christ

When given the privilege to share the Gospel, the deacon should always be patient and give a thorough presentation of the Gospel.

He should never feel as though he must rush back into the church to announce the person's decision. He must be sure to thoroughly present the fact that all are sinners who fall short of God's glory. He should share several Scriptures related to the atonement of Jesus Christ for our sin and the necessity of complete reliance upon His finished work for salvation. He must always give the person an opportunity to make a decision. When dealing with a person who has learned English as a second language, he should be especially cautious to make sure he or she understands each term.

After the person prays to accept Jesus Christ as Saviour, the deacon should bring the new convert to two or three church and staff members who will rejoice with him in his decision. The deacon should be concerned for this person and encourage him to become involved in an adult Bible class in the coming days.

Baptism

When a deacon is asked to escort someone to the baptistry, he should first listen to the testimony of the baptismal candidate. If satisfactory, they can proceed to the baptistry. At Lancaster Baptist Church, baptistry workers will provide the candidate a gown and towel. The deacon will provide assistance as needed with purses, glasses, etc. (Of course, deacons' wives would escort lady baptismal candidates to the baptistry.) The deacon should review the salvation testimony and pray with the candidate before he is baptized, asking the Lord to help him live the remainder of his life for the Lord and be a good testimony of Christ and his church to others.

General Guidelines for Counseling Those Burdened with Sin

Some people who come to the altar during the invitation are burdened with sin or a trial. The deacon should ask the Holy Spirit to help him be very sensitive to the burden of the person's heart and should avoid being judgmental of a person who is showing repentance at the altar.

The deacon may want to write down specific verses the individual can use that will help him find a way of escape should the temptation come again (see page 82). The deacon should pray with the individual and ask God for victory in his life. In cases of habitual temptation and sin, the deacon may need to refer the person to pastoral staff for additional counseling.

The deacon should be careful to maintain confidentiality about things discussed with him at the altar.

General Guidelines for Transfers and Membership

We believe the reception of new members into the church is one of the most vital aspects of the altar work being done in churches today. At Lancaster Baptist Church, membership transfers are primarily handled by the deacons and their wives. Many churches today are often filled with members who are unsaved or unaware of the true beliefs of a Baptist church. Therefore, it is vital that a deacon be prepared to ask questions adequately at the membership interview time.

First, the deacon asks the potential member to relate his salvation testimony. If he has never received Christ as his Saviour, the deacon should share the Gospel with him and give him an opportunity to trust Christ.

Once a clear testimony is given, the deacon asks the potential member about baptism. If he was biblically baptized after his salvation (see chapter 10), the deacon will complete a membership transfer form (see Appendix 7 for a sample form). If the person needs to be scripturally baptized, the deacon will explain baptism and either escort him to the baptistry or arrange to meet him at an upcoming service.

If the person has a clear salvation testimony and has been scripturally baptized, he is ready to be voted into the church. The deacon gives the completed membership transfer form to the pastor to announce to the church family.

Completing a Decision Card

At Lancaster Baptist Church, altar workers complete decision cards for every decision made during the invitations. These cards are recorded and kept in the church office as an official record of the decisions made. (See Appendix 7 for a sample card.)

Decision cards should be completed by an adult, using a pen, in printed, clear handwriting. One decision card should be completed for each person making a decision. (If a husband and wife are both saved at the same time, two decision cards should be filled out. This helps for filing and future retrieval.) Each blank on the decision card is important for follow-up, and the card should be completely filled out.

Our decision cards also have a place for the counselor to write his name so he can be contacted if there are any questions.

Scriptures for Counseling

The following list of Scripture references are sorted by topic to aid deacons in altar work. (This is also a helpful list for discipleship.)

The counseling process: put off/renew/put on

1. Confess and forsake (God alone)—Proverbs 28:13; 1 John 1:9
2. Restitution made (God and man)—Acts 24:16; Matthew 5:23–25

3. Radical amputation planned (cut sin off at its source)
    —Matthew 5:28–30; Colossians 3:5–7
4. Accountability in place—Ecclesiastes 4:9–12; Proverbs 27:5–6
5. Replacement—Romans 12:21; 13:14

ADDICTIONS
Proverbs 20:1; Isaiah 61:1; John 8:32; Romans 6:14–16; 8:2;
1 Corinthians 6:9–11; 9:26–27; Galatians 5:1

ANGER
Psalm 37:8; Proverbs 14:17,29; 15:1; 16:32; 19:11; 22:24–25;
Ecclesiastes 7:9; Ephesians 4:26,31; Colossians 3:8; James 1:19–20

APATHY
Romans 12:11; 1 Corinthians 10:31; Philippians 2:5; Colossians 3:23;
Revelation 3:15–16

ASSURANCE
John 1:12; 10:27–28; Romans 4:20–21; 8:16–17; 8:38–39; 10:13;
Philippians 1:6; 2 Timothy 1:12; Hebrews 12:6–8; 1 Peter 1:4–5;
1 John 3:20–21; 4:13–16; 5:13

AUTHORITY
Romans 13:1–4; Hebrews 13:17; 1 Peter 2:18

PARENTS
Exodus 20:12; Proverbs 20:20; 30:17; Ephesians 6:1; Colossians 3:20

BITTERNESS
Proverbs 26:24–26; Matthew 5:23–24; Luke 23:34; Ephesians 4:31;
Hebrews 12:15; James 3:14–15; 1 John 2:9–11; 3:15

BOLDNESS
Proverbs 28:1; Matthew 5:14–15; Romans 8:31; 2 Timothy 3:12;
Hebrews 13:6

COMPLAINING
Numbers 11:1; Psalm 34:1; Philippians 2:14; Hebrews 13:5

CONTENTMENT
Exodus 20:17; Proverbs 23:4–5; Matthew 6:19–24; Luke 12:15;
Ephesians 5:3; Philippians 2:21; 4:11; Colossians 3:5–6;
1 Timothy 6:6–8; Hebrews 13:5

CURSING
Exodus 20:7; Psalm 19:14; Matthew 12:34–37; Ephesians 4:29; 5:3–4;
James 3

DATING
Romans 13:14; 1 Corinthians 6:19; 2 Corinthians 6:14; Ephesians 6:1;
1 Thessalonians 4:3–7; 5:22; 2 Timothy 2:22

DEDICATION
Romans 12:1–2; Philippians 1:20–21

DEPRESSION
Psalm 32:1–7; Isaiah 40:27–31; Matthew 6:34; 11:28–30; Luke 12:22–32;
Romans 4:20–21; 2 Corinthians 4:8–9; Philippians 2:2,21;
1 Peter 5:6–7

DEVOTIONS
Joshua 1:8; Psalm 1:1–2; 19:14; 63:1; 119:9–11; Proverbs 8:17;
Jeremiah 29:13–14a; Acts 17:11; 2 Corinthians 3:18; Ephesians 4:22–24;
2 Timothy 2:15; James 1:21–25

DIVORCE
Matthew 5:31–32; 19:2–9; Luke 16:18; 1 Corinthians 7:10–15

DRINKING
Proverbs 20:1; 23:31–32; Habakkuk 2:15; Romans 6:14,16; 8:2;
1 Corinthians 6:9–11; 9:26–27; Galatians 5:1; Ephesians 5:15–18

ENVY

Proverbs 14:30; 23:17; 24:1; 1 Corinthians 13:4; Galatians 5:26; James 3:14–16; 5:9; 1 Peter 2:1–3

FORGIVENESS (GOD FORGIVES ME)

Psalm 32:1–5; 51:17; 103:12; 130:3–4; Isaiah 1:18; 55:6–7; Ephesians 4:32; Colossians 1:13–14; Hebrews 10:17; 1 John 1:9

FORGIVENESS (I FORGIVE OTHERS)

Matthew 6:14–15; 18:21–25; Mark 11:25; 2 Corinthians 2:7–8; Ephesians 4:31–32

FRIENDS (GOOD)

Psalm 119:63; Proverbs 13:20; 17:17; 18:24; 27:17

FRIENDS (BAD)

Psalm 1:1; Proverbs 13:20; 22:24–25; 24:21; 1 Corinthians 5:11; 2 Corinthians 6:14; Ephesians 5:11

GOD'S WILL

Psalm 40:8; 85:13; 130:5; Proverbs 3:5–6; Matthew 6:33; 2 Timothy 3:15–17

GOSSIP

Psalm 101:5; Proverbs 4:24; 10:18; 11:11–13; 17:9; 20:19; 21:23; Romans 1:28–29,32; Ephesians 4:29

GRATEFULNESS

Psalm 95:2; Luke 2:38; Ephesians 5:20; Colossians 3:15; 2 Thessalonians 1:3

HOMESICKNESS

Deuteronomy 31:6; Psalm 37:39–40; Isaiah 41:10; Philippians 2:3–5; 2 Timothy 1:7; 1 John 4:18

HOMOSEXUALITY
Leviticus 18:22; Matthew 19:4–5; Romans 1:26–27,32;
1 Corinthians 6:9–11; Jude 7–8

LAZINESS
Proverbs 6:6–11; 15:19; 19:15; 24:30–34; Colossians 3:23;
1 Corinthians 10:31

LUSTFUL THINKING
Proverbs 6:24–25; Matthew 5:27–28; Romans 13:14;
1 Corinthians 9:27; 10:6; Galatians 5:16; Ephesians 4:22;
2 Timothy 2:22; Titus 2:11–12; James 1:14; 1 Peter 1:14–16

LYING
Exodus 20:16; Psalm 52:1–4; Proverbs 6:16–19; 12:19,22; John 8:44;
Ephesians 4:25; Colossians 3:9

MUSIC
Psalm 40:3; 66:1–2; Romans 1:29–32; Ephesians 5:19;
Philippians 4:8; Colossians 3:16; 1 John 2:15

PEER PRESSURE
Exodus 23:2; Proverbs 1:10; 13:20; Daniel 1:8; 3:12,16–18; 6:10

PRIDE
Proverbs 6:16–18; 8:13; 11:2; 16:5,18; Daniel 4:37; Luke 18:14;
Romans 12:3; 2 Corinthians 10:5; Galatians 6:3; James 1:17; 4:6;
1 Peter 5:6

SECRET SINS
Psalm 90:8; 101:3–7; Proverbs 4:23; 15:3; Ecclesiastes 12:14; Luke 8:17

SELFISHNESS
Matthew 22:36–40; 1 Corinthians 13:4–8; Philippians 2:3–4; 2:21;
2 Timothy 3:2–5; Hebrews 3:13

TELEVISION (MOVIES)
Proverbs 14:9; Romans 1:29–32; 2 Corinthians 11:3; Ephesians 5:16;
Philippians 4:8

THOUGHT LIFE
Psalm 19:14; 101:3; Isaiah 26:3; Ezekiel 11:5; Matthew 5:27–30;
2 Corinthians 10:5; Philippians 4:8; 2 Timothy 2:22

TONGUE
Psalm 39:1; Ephesians 4:29; 5:3–4; Colossians 4:6

TRUSTING GOD
Deuteronomy 32:4; Psalm 20:7; 56:3; 62:8; 118:8; Proverbs 3:5–6;
Isaiah 26:3–4; 41:10; 50:10; Jeremiah 29:11; Lamentations 3:22–23;
Daniel 2:21

WITNESSING
Psalm 126:5–6; Proverbs 11:30; Matthew 28:19–20; Mark 16:15;
Acts 1:8; Romans 1:16; 10:13–15

WORRY
Deuteronomy 33:27; Psalm 55:22; Isaiah 41:10; Matthew 6:34;
Luke 12:22–32; Romans 4:20–21; Philippians 4:6; 2 Timothy 1:7;
1 Peter 5:7; 1 John 4:18

SALVATION
1. Realize you are a sinner—Romans 3:9–10,23; 5:12
2. Sin separates us from God—Luke 13:27; Romans 6:23a;
   Revelation 21:27
3. Works cannot get us to Heaven—Isaiah 64:6a;
   Ephesians 2:8–9; Titus 3:5
4. Turn from your sin—Mark 1:14–15; Luke 13:3; Acts 3:19
5. Trust that Jesus died for you—Luke 19:10; John 3:16–17;
   Acts 4:12; 16:31; Romans 5:8–9; 6:23b; 2 Corinthians 5:21

6. Take the free gift—John 1:12; 14:6; 20:31; Romans 5:17; 10:9–10, 13
7. Assurance—John 1:12; 10:27–28; 1 John 3:20–21; 4:13–16; 5:13

CHAPTER TEN

Understanding and Explaining Baptism

I n our last chapter, we briefly covered several common needs of those who come to the altar during a church invitation. In this chapter, we will expand on the matter of baptism. Much confusion abounds today regarding scriptural baptism, thus it is imperative that those who explain it to others have a thorough understanding themselves.

The word *baptize* appears one hundred times in the New Testament. We first learn of baptism during the preaching ministry of John the Baptist as he challenged his fellow Jews to turn from their sin to God. Baptism was their opportunity to demonstrate the genuineness of their changed heart.

Naturally, John was surprised when Jesus came to be baptized. Jesus explained that this was part of His plan. And from that day forward, baptism was the way Christ's followers would identify with Him, with His people, and with His message.

*Then cometh Jesus from Galilee to Jordan unto John, to be baptized of him. But John forbad him, saying, I have need to be baptized of thee, and comest thou to me? And Jesus answering said unto him, Suffer it to be so now: for thus it becometh us to fulfil all righteousness. Then he suffered him. And Jesus, when he was baptized, went up straightway out of the water: and, lo, the heavens were opened unto him, and he saw the Spirit of God descending like a dove, and lighting upon him: And lo a voice from heaven, saying, This is my beloved Son, in whom I am well pleased.—*MATTHEW 3:13–17

Baptism Is a Means of Identification

In its most basic sense, baptism is a mark of identification. When we are baptized, it identifies us in three ways:

First, baptism identifies us with the Lord Jesus Christ.

As Jesus proclaimed Himself as the Messiah from God, many responded by embracing His message. Baptism was an opportunity for new believers—both then and now—to go public with their decision to follow Jesus Christ. Like a wedding ring identifies a wife with her husband, so baptism identifies Christians with their Lord. Matthew 28:19 says, *"Go ye therefore, and teach all nations, baptizing them in the name of the Father, and of the Son, and of the Holy Ghost."*

Baptism pictures Christ's death on the Cross, His burial, and His resurrection from the grave. This reminds us that, when we are born again in salvation, our former life is buried with Christ, and a new life is raised in its place (2 Corinthians 5:17).

Second, baptism identifies us with an assembly of believers.

After Christ's ascension, the good news of the Gospel spread, and new believers began to assemble and organize as churches. When individuals received Christ, baptism identified them with the other believers in their city. When someone was baptized, in the presence of their fellow believers, they were in essence saying to their neighbors, "I'm with them!"

Describing those saved at Pentecost, Acts 2:41 says, *"Then they that gladly received his word were baptized: and the same day there were added unto them about three thousand souls."*

Third, baptism identifies us with a body of teaching.

When someone was baptized, they were not only identifying with a group of people, but also with the doctrine held by that group.

Those who were baptized on the day of Pentecost *"...continued stedfastly in the apostles' doctrine and fellowship, and in breaking of bread, and in prayers"* (Acts 2:42).

Matthew 28:19–20 commands us to not only give people the Gospel, but to baptize them and teach them Bible doctrine: *"Go ye therefore, and teach all nations, baptizing them in the name of the Father, and of the Son, and of the Holy Ghost: Teaching them to observe all things whatsoever I have commanded you: and, lo, I am with you alway, even unto the end of the world. Amen."*

Throughout the first century, church leaders and New Testament writers emphasized the importance of doctrinal accuracy and unity. The conviction of the apostles was that doctrinal soundness was a critical factor in Christian fellowship. (See 1 Corinthians 1:10; Philippians 1:27; 1 Timothy 1:3, 10, 4:13, 16; 2 Timothy 3:16, 4:2–3; Titus 2:1; 2 John 10; and Jude 3.)

Three Biblical Criteria for Baptism

There are three criteria found in the New Testament, for the important step of baptism:

First, the order of baptism is after conversion.

Baptism was not intended for those who have not yet personally received Christ. God's design is for us to first make our own decision to accept His gift, and then to follow Him in baptism. Baptism is an outward expression of a decision that has already occurred in our hearts.

After the Ethiopian eunuch trusted Christ, he wanted to be baptized. It is significant to note that Philip emphasized that baptism was not part of salvation, but an expression of it. Acts 8:36–37 says, *"And as they went on their way, they came unto a certain water: and the eunuch said, See, here is water; what doth hinder me to be baptized? And Philip said, If thou believest with all thine heart, thou mayest. And he answered and said, I believe that Jesus Christ is the Son of God."*

Second, the mode of baptism is immersion.

The language used in the New Testament indicates that the baptisms of the first century were by immersion (Matthew 3:16, John 3:23). In fact the word baptize literally means "to plunge, dunk, or submerge." Only immersion properly pictures the death, burial and resurrection of Christ.

Scripture is clear that when Philip baptized the Ethiopian eunuch, he did so by immersion. Acts 8:38 tells us, *"And he commanded the chariot to stand still: and they went down both into the water, both Philip and the eunuch; and he baptized him."*

Third, the authority of baptism is the local church.

Local churches have been given the responsibility to carry out two ordinances: Baptism and the Lord's Table (sometimes called Communion). These reminders of Christ's redemptive work were not given to the general community at large. They were entrusted to local churches, to be carried out in the context of local, personal ministry.

It would be impossible to keep track of biblical soundness and doctrinal purity at a global level, but they can be observed locally. The Apostle Paul indicated that the institution of the local church serves as a foundation, which supports God's truth: *"But if I tarry long, that thou mayest know how thou oughtest to behave thyself in the house of God, which is the church of the living God, the pillar and ground of the truth"* (1 Timothy 3:15)

God has entrusted pastors with the responsibility of overseeing His local congregations (Acts 20:28, 1 Peter 5:2). Each pastor is accountable to God for the spiritual health of the church he serves. When folks identify with a church's doctrine through baptism, they are assisting the pastor in maintaining doctrinal purity and unity.

Baptism Serves as a Testimony

Baptism testifies of my relationship with and devotion to my Saviour.

Someone who knows and loves the Lord enjoys letting others know. Just as a newly married man is happy to display his wedding band, it's natural for a Christian to give testimony of his relationship with Jesus Christ. *"For the scripture saith, Whosoever believeth on him shall not be ashamed"* (Romans 10:11).

Baptism testifies of my unity and agreement with my church family.

In recent years, some churches have downplayed the importance of doctrine. But we want to be on the same page as those with whom we are worshiping, growing, and serving. A church unified in doctrine is able to move forward, accomplishing much more for Christ's cause than one where disharmony and confusion are present.

Paul wrote to the Corinthian church, *"Now I beseech you, brethren, by the name of our Lord Jesus Christ, that ye all speak the same thing, and that there be no divisions among you; but that ye be perfectly joined together in the same mind and in the same judgment"* (1 Corinthians 1:10).

Sometimes folks will come to Lancaster Baptist from another denomination or doctrinal background, and yet feel that God is leading them to unite—in faith and service—with our church. In this case, being baptized simply communicates to the church family this person's commitment to doctrinal unity. It lets our assembly know, "I'm with you in doctrine and in spirit!"

We read in Acts 19:1–7, that Paul baptized twelve men who had previously been baptized by John the Baptist. The reason for this baptism was to identify with the current, New Testament doctrine, which Paul preached.

Those who have recently received Christ as Saviour should not hesitate to identify with Him through baptism. It is their first step of obedience. Jesus said, *"Ye are my friends, if ye do whatsoever I command you"* (John 15:14).

CHAPTER ELEVEN

Church Discipline

The very idea of leadership implies the role of responsibility. A leader goes before and shows the way, thus he must know what to do and when to do it. And he must assume the responsibility for its timing and completion.

One of the more difficult responsibilities of leadership is dealing with defiance in the church—lovingly confronting those who are living in a way that is harmful to the church body. Yet, this aspect of leadership is necessary for the spiritual health of the flock.

First Peter 5:8 warns, *"Be sober, be vigilant; because your adversary the devil, as a roaring lion, walketh about, seeking whom he may devour."* The adversary constantly stalks Christians' lives and homes, specially targeting them for his destruction.

The process of church discipline is one way pastors can counter Satan's attacks in the church. This God-given responsibility of spiritual leaders is designed for the spiritual benefit of those who have become victims of Satan's attacks and to protect the rest of the flock from becoming prey.

While the primary responsibility of church discipline falls on the pastor, deacons will sometimes be asked to assist in this process. At our church, two deacons serve as a "discipline committee" to assist me as needed in these matters. (See Appendix 4 for brief committee description.)

The Purpose of Discipline

Throughout the New Testament, God gives several purposes for disciplinary intervention in the life of a believer:

For the believer's profit—Our Heavenly Father's corrective measures are always for our benefit. His correction when we sin is proof of His love; He protects us from the harm we would bring upon ourselves. Hebrews 12:10 says, *"For they verily for a few days chastened us after their own pleasure; but he for our profit, that we might be partakers of his holiness."*

To restore a brother—Church discipline provides for the spiritual restoration of one who has fallen in sin. Galatians 6:1 admonishes, *"Brethren, if a man be overtaken in a fault, ye which are spiritual, restore such an one in the spirit of meekness; considering thyself, lest thou also be tempted."*

Paul wrote of the godly repentance the church of Corinth expressed after Paul's disciplinary epistle of 2 Corinthians: *"For behold this selfsame thing, that ye sorrowed after a godly sort, what carefulness it wrought in you, yea, what clearing of yourselves, yea, what indignation, yea, what fear, yea, what vehement desire, yea, what zeal, yea, what revenge! In all things ye have approved yourselves to be clear in this matter"* (2 Corinthians 7:11).

To protect the assembly—When one member of the church persists in a rebellious spirit or flaunts his sin, it damages weaker Christians in the church. Church discipline helps to clear the confusion in the hearts of young Christians and protects the church from the loss of more lives. In 1 Timothy 5:20 Paul instructs, *"Them that sin rebuke before all, that others also may fear."* (See also 2 Thessalonians 3:6–7, 14–15.)

To remove the defilement of sin—First Corinthians 5:6 explains, *"A little leaven leaveneth the whole lump."* Even so, a little sin in any person's life brings defilement and could eventually defile the whole church body. When a church member practices open, flagrant sin and refuses to repent after being approached by the pastor, this will bring defilement to the church. (Examples of such sins would include adultery, pregnancy out of wedlock, public drunkenness or illicit drug use, and being arrested for moral crimes.) Church discipline cleanses the church of having a part in the sin as they corporately express their desire for the offender's repentance and restoration.

To deliver to Satan for the destruction of the flesh—When a Christian will not respond to the first steps of church discipline, the church must dismiss that person from their membership. First Corinthians 5:5 explains the reason for this: *"To deliver such an one unto Satan for the destruction of the flesh, that the spirit may be saved in the day of the Lord Jesus."* The man referred to in this passage was living in gross immorality (1 Corinthians 5:1). Paul instructed the Corinthian church that it would be better for this man to be released from the spiritual protection of membership that he might experience the full effects of his sin.

Even this weighty step in church discipline is executed with the hope of repentance. Thankfully, 2 Corinthians 2:6–7 records the godly sorrow wrought in this man's heart through church discipline. Paul now instructs the church to restore him to membership and to encourage spiritual growth: *"Sufficient to such a man is this punishment, which was inflicted of many. So that contrariwise ye ought rather to forgive him, and comfort him, lest perhaps such a one should be swallowed up with overmuch sorrow."*

The purpose of discipline is never for personal vindication. This difficult responsibility of church leadership is administered with a heart of loving compassion and a desire for restoration and spiritual growth and fruit.

The Process of Discipline

The process of church discipline is primarily the pastor's responsibility and should be handled according to his discretion. Although he may ask the deacons to assist him in this process, how and when to deal with it is at his discernment.

Matthew 18 and Galatians 6 both speak to the matter of church discipline, and both passages emphasize a loving, restorative spirit. This is a process that must be handled with humility and grace.

Deal with it as privately as possible—Sometimes, a backslidden church member simply needs a concerned pastor to personally and lovingly confront him of his sin. Matthew 18:15 points to this private meeting as the first step of correction: *"Moreover if thy brother shall trespass against thee, go and tell him his fault between thee and him alone: if he shall hear thee, thou hast gained thy brother."*

Even if the church member does not respond to the first step, the matter is still to be dealt with as privately as possible. The next step, often involving one or two deacons, is still a private meeting of only a few people: *"But if he will not hear thee, then take with thee one or two more, that in the mouth of two or three witnesses every word may be established"* (Matthew 18:16).

It is only after every effort has been made for private repentance that the matter must be brought before the church: *"And if he shall neglect to hear them, tell it unto the church: but if he neglect to hear the church, let him be unto thee as an heathen man and a publican"* (Matthew 18:17).

Let them go—We noted earlier Paul's instruction to the Corinthian church to dismiss one of their members who blatantly rejected godliness. In 1 Timothy 1:20, Paul writes of another case in which he had to remove the spiritual protection of fellowship because of two men's refusal of truth: *"Of whom is Hymenaeus and Alexander; whom I have delivered unto Satan, that they may learn not to blaspheme."* If a Christian will not repent, the church must release him from membership. This level of church discipline is very painful for the pastor and the church family, but it emphasizes the severity of sin to both the offender and the rest of the church family; its very severity urges repentance.

Remove yourself from them—Apparently, Hymenaeus never did repent, for we read of him again in 2 Timothy 2:16–19: *"But shun profane and vain babblings: for they will increase unto more ungodliness. And their word will eat as doth a canker: of whom is Hymenaeus and Philetus; Who concerning the truth have erred, saying that the resurrection is past already; and overthrow the faith of some. Nevertheless the foundation of God standeth sure, having this seal, The Lord knoweth them that are his. And, Let every one that nameth the name of Christ depart from iniquity."* In this passage, Paul notes that the doctrinal error Hymenaeus and Philetus insisted on promoting in the church was overthrowing the faith of others. For this reason, he instructed Timothy to encourage the church to depart from this iniquity.

In 1 Timothy 6:3–5, Paul also wrote of the need to withdraw from unruly men who reject biblical truth: *"If any man teach otherwise, and consent not to wholesome words, even the words of our Lord Jesus Christ, and to the doctrine which is according to godliness; He is proud, knowing nothing, but doting about questions and strifes of words, whereof cometh envy, strife, railings, evil surmisings, Perverse disputings of men of corrupt minds, and destitute of the truth, supposing that gain is godliness: from such withdraw thyself."*

Titus 3:10–11 commands, *"A man that is an heretick after the first and second admonition reject; Knowing that he that is such is subverted, and sinneth, being condemned of himself."* This final step of church discipline relates primarily to people who cause division and undermine the faith of others through propagating doctrinal error. It is only taken after earlier steps have been attempted.

It is important to note that the process of church discipline applies only to those who are desiring to stay in the church but are continuing in sin. If a member has already fallen out of church, discipline is not relevant for he has already removed himself from the spiritual protection of the church. (According to the constitution of a particular church, he will be removed from the active membership role to an inactive role, and then eventually removed altogether.) A backslidden Christian who leaves the church on his own needs his church family to reach out to him in love and encourage him to return to the Lord.

Author and teacher, Dr. Howard Hendricks tells the story of a young man who strayed from the Lord but was finally brought back by the help of a friend who really loved him. When there was full repentance and restoration, Dr. Hendricks asked this Christian how it felt away from the Lord. The young man said it seemed like he was out at sea, in deep water, deep trouble, and all his friends were on the shore hurling biblical accusations at him about justice, penalty, and wrong. "But, there was one Christian brother who actually swam out to get me and would not let me go. I fought him, but he pushed aside my fighting, grasped me, put a life jacket around me, and took me to shore. By the grace of God, he was the reason I was restored. He would not let me go."

This is the spirit each of us should have toward those who are in sin. While full restoration cannot take place until genuine repentance is expressed, we should be willing to "swim out" to those who are sinking in sin—whether through the process of church discipline or seeking to bring back a brother who has fallen away from the church.

Restore the repentant member—Because the purpose of church discipline is restoration, churches must be ready to restore the fallen church member after church discipline. Paul actually rebuked the Corinthian church for their failure to restore their fallen brother (2 Corinthians 2:6–7). Their eagerness to follow Paul's instructions had become harshness in not affirming their love to their now repentant brother. In 2 Corinthians 2:8, Paul wrote, *"Wherefore I beseech you that ye would confirm your love toward him."*

Galatians 6 emphasizes the need for a restorative church, a church who is willing to receive and accept a member back into the church after repentance. Verse 1 says, *"Brethren, if a man be overtaken in a fault, ye which are spiritual, restore such an one in the spirit of meekness; considering thyself, lest thou also be tempted."*

The first step for restoration must be repentance, for you cannot restore an unrepentant sinner. In 2 Corinthians 7, Paul distinguishes between the worldly sorrow that regrets only the consequences of sin and the godly sorrow that grieves over the sin itself. This godly sorrow is the true repentance necessary for restoration: *"For godly sorrow worketh repentance to salvation not to be repented of: but the sorrow of the world worketh death"* (2 Corinthians 7:10).

When a fallen member desires to be reinstated to the church membership, he should first meet with the pastor and some of the deacons. He will then come before the church, and he or the pastor will express his repentance and desire to once again be part of the church.

The church family should freely forgive their brother. If the person has wronged individuals or the congregation, he should make whatever restitution is possible.

The process of full restoration may involve some ongoing personal counseling, accountability, and restrictive activity in the church until the member is once again spiritually grounded and living in consistent spiritual victory.

The Pursuit of Discipline

If a church leader involved in the process of church discipline acts from a heart of anger, frustration, or impatience, the offender will sense this, and the process will be thwarted. James 1:20 says, *"For the wrath of man worketh not the righteousness of God."*

Three words describe the heart in which a church leader should carry out church discipline when necessary:

Prayer—Only God knows the full situation, including the motives and influences involved. Wise church leaders spend much time seeking God's wisdom in the specifics of church discipline. James 1:5 encourages, *"If any of you lack wisdom, let him ask of God, that giveth to all men liberally, and upbraideth not; and it shall be given him."*

Patience—When a pastor or church leader rushes into church discipline without God's wisdom and having researched the details as carefully as possible, he is acting independently of God's Spirit. Second Timothy 2:24–26 says, *"And the servant of the Lord must not strive; but be gentle unto all men, apt to teach, patient, In meekness instructing those that oppose themselves; if God peradventure will give them repentance to the acknowledging of the truth; And that they may recover themselves out of the snare of the devil, who are taken captive by him at his will."* We must exercise great patience and gentleness as we firmly deal with the sin in people's lives.

Partner—When issues arise that I believe require church discipline, I have often been helped by seeking the counsel of pastor friends and the deacons on our discipline committee. Their spiritual support has greatly aided me during these difficult times. (Of course, when seeking counsel, one must be very careful to retain confidentiality where needed.)

Proverbs 15:22 says *"Without counsel purposes are disappointed: but in the multitude of counsellors they are established."* Because the purpose of church discipline—reaching the heart and conscience of the offender—is crucial to its success, I want to seek counsel that will help to establish and accomplish this purpose. This is not about merely completing a process; it is about reaching the heart of a precious member of the flock.

Years ago, a man rushed into the Rijksmuseum and attacked the valuable painting, *The Nightwatch,* with a bread knife. This work of art, completed in 1642 by Rembrandt, was slashed in a zig-zag pattern and appeared destroyed. Yet, immediately, restorers set to work on it. Although some evidence of the vandalism is still evident up close, the workmen were remarkably successful. As quickly as possible, the painting was returned to its display in the museum.

In similar fashion to the painting's attacker, Satan assaults Christians. Like a ruthless vandal, he slashes their ministry and destroys their lives through sin. God has given church leaders the privilege and responsibility of restoring these lives through the ministry of church discipline. *"Brethren, if a man be overtaken in a fault, ye which are spiritual, restore such an one…"* (Galatians 6:1).

CHAPTER TWELVE

Ministering the Lord's Table

D eacons are often asked to serve the Lord's Table to the congregation. This chapter outlines the purposes of the Lord's Table and provides Scriptures that will encourage you to have a prepared heart, ready to serve it to the church family.

> "For I have received of the Lord that which also I delivered unto you, That the Lord Jesus the same night in which he was betrayed took bread: And when he had given thanks, he brake it, and said, Take, eat: this is my body, which is broken for you: this do in remembrance of me. After the same manner also he took the cup, when he had supped, saying, This cup is the new testament in my blood: this do ye, as oft as ye drink it, in remembrance of me. For as often as ye eat this bread, and drink this cup, ye do shew the Lord's death till he come. Wherefore whosoever shall eat this

bread, and drink this cup of the Lord, unworthily, shall be guilty of the body and blood of the Lord. But let a man examine himself, and so let him eat of that bread, and drink of that cup. For he that eateth and drinketh unworthily, eateth and drinketh damnation to himself, not discerning the Lord's body. For this cause many are weak and sickly among you, and many sleep. For if we would judge ourselves, we should not be judged. But when we are judged, we are chastened of the Lord, that we should not be condemned with the world. Wherefore, my brethren, when ye come together to eat, tarry one for another. And if any man hunger, let him eat at home; that ye come not together unto condemnation. And the rest will I set in order when I come."—1 CORINTHIANS 11:23–34

Christ instituted two ordinances for His church—baptism and the Lord's Supper. Both ordinances point to Christ and remind us of the great price He paid for our salvation.

As Bible-believing Baptists, we do not refer to these ordinances as "sacraments," for they in no way pay for our salvation. We praise God that we are not saved by works but by grace through faith. We observe the Lord's Supper, not hoping to receive salvation, but choosing to remember our Saviour who already purchased our salvation.

Under the teaching of the Roman Catholic church, when a priest administers the wafer and wine of communion, the recipient believes he is receiving Christ's literal, physical body and blood. And he believes that this act is a part of his salvation. This doctrine, called *transubstantiation*, is not taught in Scripture. The Bible gives an entirely different teaching on the Lord's Supper.

The Lord's Supper was first given by Jesus to His disciples the night He was betrayed to be crucified. Knowing that He was soon to give His life as the payment for our sins, Jesus gathered His disciples together into an upper room for the Last Supper.

This occurred at the time of the Jewish Passover, which commemorated the deliverance of Israel from Egypt. Exodus 7–12 records the plagues God released on Egypt when Pharaoh refused to allow God's people to depart. The final plague was to be the death of the firstborn. In one night, the death angel would go through Egypt and kill every firstborn. But God made provision by which the Hebrews could be spared from this plague. They were to kill a lamb and apply its blood to the doorposts of their houses. God promised, *"...when he seeth the blood upon the lintel, and on the two side posts, the* LORD *will pass over the door, and will not suffer the destroyer to come in unto your houses to smite you"* (Exodus 12:23). Redemption has always been paid by a blood sacrifice—not through receiving sacraments or keeping religious traditions.

When Christ instituted the Lord's Supper with His apostles on that last Passover night, He was hours away from giving His body to be broken and His blood to be shed to pay the costly price to deliver us from sin. He wanted the apostles and future church leaders to remember the sacrifice He was about to make, so He instructed them, *"this do in remembrance of me"* (Luke 22:19). Thus, the Lord's Supper, or the Lord's Table, is not a sacrament but a remembrance. The elements do not save, but they do cause us to remember.

Questions and Answers

Q: How often should the Lord's Table be observed?

A: Some pastors observe the Lord's Table only once each year because Christ instituted it on the occasion of the Passover which was observed annually. At Lancaster Baptist Church, our custom is to have the Lord's Table a few times throughout the year. In Scripture, the emphasis of the Lord's Table is not placed on its timing, but on its reminder of Christ's sacrifice.

First Corinthians 11:26 simply says, *"For as often as ye eat this bread, and drink this cup, ye do shew the Lord's death till he come."* Thus, each pastor and church is free to decide under the Holy Spirit's direction how often to administer the Lord's Table.

Q: Where should the Lord's Table be observed?

A: The Greek word for *church* is *ecclesia*, meaning "called out assembly." When Christ instituted the Lord's Table, He gathered His disciples, whom He called out in Matthew 10, and instructed them, *"…this do in remembrance of me"* (Luke 22:19). In 1 Corinthians 11, Paul is addressing a local church, a called out group of Christians, as he gives instruction concerning the Lord's Table.

The institution of the Lord's Table was the early called-out assembly, and the instructions of administering the Lord's Table were given to the local body of Christ at Corinth. Thus, Scripture teaches that the Lord's Table is intended for the local church. Never in Scripture do we find the Lord's Table administered in a "universal church" or "global church" setting.

As Baptists, we don't observe the Lord's Table simply out of tradition, but because of biblical instruction. Notice that as Paul instructed the church in Corinth on administering the Lord's Table, he was not sharing his own ideas; he was writing under divine inspiration.

> *For I have received of the Lord that which also I delivered unto you….*— 1 CORINTHIANS 11:23

In 1 Corinthians 11, God gives us three purposes of the Lord's Table. In the following pages, we will examine them each individually.

To Remember the Lord

For I have received of the Lord that which also I delivered unto you, That the Lord Jesus the same night in which he was betrayed took bread: And when he had given thanks, he brake it, and said, Take, eat: this is my body, which is broken for you: this do in remembrance of me. After the same manner also he took the cup, when he had supped, saying, This cup is the new testament in my blood: this do ye, as oft as ye drink it, in remembrance of me.—1 CORINTHIANS 11:23–25

Our lives are inundated with that which competes for our attention. From projects at work, to needs at home, to news reports, to hobbies and outside interests, life is constantly vying for our attention. The technology of our day adds its own set of distractions as it blinks, beeps, and buzzes with a landslide of information and communication.

The Lord's Table is an opportunity to pull aside from every distraction and focus our attention solely on Christ and His sacrifice for us.

The Bread

The bread symbolizes Christ's body. Earlier Jesus stated, *"I am the bread of life."*

For the bread of God is he which cometh down from heaven, and giveth life unto the world. Then said they unto him, Lord, evermore give us this bread. And Jesus said unto them, I am the bread of life: he that cometh to me shall never hunger; and he that believeth on me shall never thirst.— JOHN 6:33–35

As Christ shared the Last Supper with His disciples in the upper room, He was ready to give His body to be beaten and crucified, and He instituted the Lord's Table that we might remember the greatness of His loving sacrifice for us. As we take the bread, it reminds us of Christ's body, broken for us.

> *And as they were eating, Jesus took bread, and blessed it, and brake it, and gave it to the disciples, and said, Take, eat; this is my body.*—MATTHEW 26:26

The Cross was a brutal scene. God in the flesh hung on the Cross with His body beaten by the Roman whip, nails driven through His hands and feet, and a crown of thorns implanted in His brow. His body was literally torn apart; His visage was marred beyond recognition (Isaiah 52:14), and every joint was ripped out of socket (Psalm 22:14).

The bread reminds us that Christ's body was broken *for us*. This supreme sacrifice was for *our* sins.

> *Surely he hath borne our griefs, and carried our sorrows: yet we did esteem him stricken, smitten of God, and afflicted. But he was wounded for our transgressions, he was bruised for our iniquities: the chastisement of our peace was upon him; and with his stripes we are healed.*—ISAIAH 53:4–5

The Cup

As the bread symbolizes Christ's body, the juice symbolizes His blood.

> *And he took the cup, and gave thanks, and gave it to them, saying, Drink ye all of it; For this is my blood of the new testament, which is shed for many for the remission of sins.*—MATTHEW 26:27–28

The blood that gushed from Jesus' broken body was the infinite, eternal payment for our sin. Christ was conceived of the Holy Ghost (Luke 1:35) and came to earth as the Son of God—God robed in human flesh. He lived a perfectly sinless life in the flesh, and while He was tempted in all points like as we are, He was without sin (Hebrews 4:15). The blood of Christ is the payment for our salvation.

We are justified by the blood.

> *Much more then, being now justified by his blood, we shall be saved from wrath through him.*
> —ROMANS 5:9

> *And almost all things are by the law purged with blood; and without shedding of blood is no remission.*
> —HEBREWS 9:22

We are washed in the blood.

> *But if we walk in the light, as he is in the light, we have fellowship one with another, and the blood of Jesus Christ his Son cleanseth us from all sin.*
> —1 JOHN 1:7

As the songwriter so clearly wrote,

> What can wash away my sin?
> Nothing but the blood of Jesus;
> What can make me whole again?
> Nothing but the blood of Jesus.
> —ROBERT LOWRY

We are purchased by the blood.

> *Take heed therefore unto yourselves, and to all the flock, over the which the Holy Ghost hath made you*

overseers, to feed the church of God, which he hath purchased with his own blood.—ACTS 20:28

The great price Christ paid for the church—His own blood—reveals the tremendous value of the local church.

We are redeemed by the blood.

In whom we have redemption through his blood, even the forgiveness of sins:—COLOSSIANS 1:14

Forgiveness for sins cannot be obtained by the baptistry water, church membership, or good works. Christ redeemed us through His blood alone. The juice reminds us that without the shedding of the blood of Christ, there would be no hope, no help, no way to Heaven.

Salvation is available because Jesus gave His body to be broken and shed His blood to pay for our sins. If you have put your faith in Him, according to the Word of God, you have been declared righteous by a holy God. Salvation is not because of what we have done but because of what Christ did for us.

Don't ever become weary of meditating on Christ's sacrifice for us. We shouldn't partake of the Lord's Table grudgingly. The great and overwhelming purpose of the Lord's Table is to remember the Lord and the love He expressed for you on the Cross. Focus your attention, gratefulness, and adoration on Him.

To Revive His Church

Wherefore whosoever shall eat this bread, and drink this cup of the Lord, unworthily, shall be guilty of the body and blood of the Lord. But let a man examine himself, and so let him eat of that bread, and drink of that cup. For he that eateth and drinketh unworthily, eateth and drinketh damnation to himself, not

discerning the Lord's body. For this cause many are
weak and sickly among you, and many sleep. For if
we would judge ourselves, we should not be judged.
—1 CORINTHIANS 11:27–31

Through the Lord's Table we remember Christ's atonement at the Cross. And when we do, we find that a fresh look at the Cross brings revival to the church. That revival comes when we obey the Lord's command to examine ourselves before partaking of the Lord's Table.

Many churches have scheduled revival meetings when extra time is set aside for services. In our church, these times have been very beneficial. But there is no need to wait for revival until the "revival services." God has designed the Lord's Table to focus our hearts on the Cross and thus bring revival. The Lord's Table should be the closest time of unity with the Lord and each other that a church experiences.

Repentance of the Heart

It has been said, "At the heart of a problem is a problem of the heart." This is why the Lord has instructed us to examine our hearts and repent of sin in our lives. The word *examine* (Greek *dokimazo*) in 1 Corinthians 11:28 means "to test, prove, or scrutinize."

Many in the Corinthian church were partaking of the Lord's Table "unworthily"—without respect. They were living in gluttony, division, lawsuits, and immorality. And in the midst of this sin, they approached the Lord's Table as if these sins (for which Christ gave His body to be broken and His blood to be shed) were of no consequence. This demonstrated great disrespect for the body of which Christ's sacrifice had made them a part—the church Jesus loved and purchased with His own blood.

Repentance begins with identifying the things in our lives that are not genuine—motives, actions, attitudes, or thoughts. If we cannot be honest in our heart of hearts with ourselves and with the Lord, then we won't repent. How grievous that would be to the Lord!

I've had a few men over the years tell me, "I know I'm not right with the Lord, so I'm not going to partake of the Lord's Table." But Christ doesn't give that as an option—He commands us to partake in remembrance of Him. He doesn't give a pass on the Lord's Table to a Christian who wants to continue in sin. Rather, one purpose of the Lord's Table is to bring Christians to a point of repentance; it is the time to deal with sin.

> *Draw nigh to God, and he will draw nigh to you. Cleanse your hands, ye sinners; and purify your hearts, ye double minded.*—JAMES 4:8

As one old farmer commented, "Many Christians spend six days a week sowing wild oats and then come to church and pray for crop failure." True repentance does not simply seek relief from the *consequences* of sin, but it turns from the *actions* of sin.

If we were to examine each other, many would happily expose the faults of their spouses or fellow church members. But notice that God commands each one to "examine himself." D.L. Moody said, "I have more trouble examining D.L. Moody than any other man I know."

Before you partake of the Lord's Table, examine your heart in light of the Cross. Be sure you are saved and that you are living a sanctified life, having repented of any known sin. Think over the past week, and back further to the last time you partook of the Lord's Table. How is your fellowship with the Lord and with other Christians? How is your growth in grace? Has some carnal habit crept back into your life? Are you at odds with a brother or sister in Christ?

God desires an *examined* heart and a *separated* heart. When we were saved, we were called as a body of believers to be separated unto Christ. Our lives are to reflect the holiness of God.

> *But sanctify the Lord God in your hearts: and be ready always to give an answer to every man that asketh you a reason of the hope that is in you with meekness and fear:—*1 PETER 3:15

The church in Corinth was surrounded by pagan, idolatrous worship, and some of the Christians in Corinth were still involved with the idolatrous services and rituals. Paul pointed out the foolishness of living their old lifestyle most of the time and then hypocritically partaking of the Lord's Table at church.

> *For we being many are one bread, and one body: for we are all partakers of that one bread. Behold Israel after the flesh: are not they which eat of the sacrifices partakers of the altar? What say I then? that the idol is any thing, or that which is offered in sacrifice to idols is any thing? But I say, that the things which the Gentiles sacrifice, they sacrifice to devils, and not to God: and I would not that ye should have fellowship with devils. Ye cannot drink the cup of the Lord, and the cup of devils: ye cannot be partakers of the Lord's table, and of the table of devils. Do we provoke the Lord to jealousy? are we stronger than he?—*1 CORINTHIANS 10:17–22

Christians today need to learn this truth—God desires complete ownership of our lives. He has a jealousy for our complete love. We cannot give true loyalty to Christ when we are choosing to enjoy sinful pleasures at the same time. To live for the world, the flesh, and the devil throughout the week and then to partake of the Lord's Table with plans to go right back to sin on Monday is a dishonor to the Lord and His love for you. The seriousness with which God regards the Lord's Table is seen in 1 Corinthians 11:30: *"For this cause many are weak and sickly among you, and many sleep."*

God has called us to be a holy people—a people whose lifestyle proclaims His greatness.

> *But ye are a chosen generation, a royal priesthood, an holy nation, a peculiar people; that ye should shew forth the praises of him who hath called you out of darkness into his marvellous light: Which in time past were not a people, but are now the people of God: which had not obtained mercy, but now have obtained mercy. Dearly beloved, I beseech you as strangers and pilgrims, abstain from fleshly lusts, which war against the soul;*—1 PETER 2:9–11

The world is looking for people whose lives stand out for Christ. Don't be ashamed of Him; gladly live for Him.

Notice in 1 Corinthians 11:27 that we are not to take the Lord's Supper "unworthily." It is only the blood of Christ that makes us worthy to partake of the Lord's Table. Thus, only Christians should partake.

Sometimes it's difficult for a pastor, especially a young pastor coming into an established church, to follow God's instructions as to who should partake of the Lord's Table. The first time I administered the Lord's Table at Lancaster Baptist Church was in 1986. Before administering the Lord's Table, I explained that this ordinance was for the local body and that it was only for those who were saved and members of Lancaster Baptist Church. I requested that, while those who were not saved should feel free to watch, they would please not participate.

There were fifteen people in attendance, including Earl and Judy Farar. Earl was a serious-looking man with gray beginning to speckle his hair. Judy was a dear lady who had been praying for her husband's salvation for many years. Being young and inexperienced, I was nervous about publicly asking those who were not saved (which would include Earl) not to partake, but I knew this was the stand that the Lord had convicted me was right.

After the service, Earl came directly to me, grabbed my arm, and said, "I need to talk to you." As I led him to my office, I was sure this was going to be a difficult conversation.

After we seated ourselves, Earl simply said, "I'm ready."

I was taken aback and hoped he didn't mean he was ready for a fight. "You are?" I questioned.

"Yes, I'm ready to be saved."

I had shared the Gospel with him several times in the past, but it was through my stand on the administration of the Lord's Table that he saw his need for salvation. I had the privilege of leading Earl to the Lord that night—Christmas Eve. God blesses His work done His way.

Revival of the Church

The repentance of individual hearts will affect the entire church body. When 1 Corinthians 11:27 notes the importance of discerning *"the Lord's body,"* I believe Paul is referring to both the physical body of the Lord and the body of the church. Even as we discern and remember Christ's broken physical body, we discern and respect the local church body.

Around the turn of the twentieth century, many Baptist churches had a "church covenant" in addition to their doctrinal statement. To join the church, a prospective member had to agree to this covenant in which they promised to pray for other members, be faithful to church, stop discord, refrain from using or selling any intoxicating beverages, and other similar things.

Churches who used a church covenant would often have a "covenant meeting" before partaking of the Lord's Table. They would read the covenant aloud and encourage the members to search their hearts to be sure they had been faithfully upholding the scripturally-based promises they had made to the local church. In this way, the church was taking care to respect the body of Christ—the local church.

In our text, Paul gives an illustration of the importance of the church body coming in unity to partake of the Lord's Table.

> *Now in this that I declare unto you I praise you not, that ye come together not for the better, but for the worse. For first of all, when ye come together in the church, I hear that there be divisions among you; and I partly believe it. For there must be also heresies among you, that they which are approved may be made manifest among you.*—1 CORINTHIANS 11:17–19

When we examine our hearts by the Word of God, the Holy Spirit is free to work in the church. Specifically, proper respect to the Lord's Table by careful examination prevents the spread of division or false doctrine.

I believe Scripture indicates a selective and protective administration of the Lord's Table. Thus, I prefer a closed Lord's Table in which only saved, baptized members of a particular local church may partake. Consider the following reasons:

The context of 1 Corinthians 11 is a local church

Paul's instructions concerning the Lord's Table were written to a local church body. It is in this context that God-ordained spiritual accountability flourishes.

To promote unity in the local church

I do not believe that the privilege of partaking in the Lord's Table belongs to someone who is disobedient to the Lord's command of baptism or who has not committed himself as a member of a local church. Membership has both responsibilities and privileges—partaking of the Lord's Table is one of the privileges.

To preserve doctrine

By partaking of the Lord's Table, we are promoting the doctrine of the atoning work of Christ. Before someone joins our church, we hear his testimony of salvation, but we often have no idea of a visitor's salvation testimony.

To prevent a pastor from usurping pastoral authority over another man's flock

I do not want to assume authority over someone else, especially a member from another church of like faith. I believe the Lord's Table is a local church ordinance. Thus I do not serve the Lord's Table to members of another church, as I believe to do so I would be shepherding another man's flock.

For example, Lancaster Baptist Church is the home of West Coast Baptist College. In some circumstances, pastors who send their students to WCBC ask the students to keep their home church membership, sometimes because they want them to reserve participation of the Lord's Table for their home church. I never want to come between a pastor and his student by usurping his authority.

To promote the authority of the local church regarding church discipline

According to Matthew 18, the local church is God's highest institution on earth in spiritual authority. Suppose someone is not in right fellowship with his church, or perhaps he has even been dismissed from his church. If he comes to Lancaster Baptist Church when we are serving the Lord's Table, I would likely have no idea of this situation. If I allowed him to partake, I would be negating the authority of the discipline administered by his local church.

First Corinthians 5 gives an illustration of church discipline in relation to the Lord's Table.

It is reported commonly that there is fornication among you, and such fornication as is not so much as named among the Gentiles, that one should have his father's wife. And ye are puffed up, and have not rather mourned, that he that hath done this deed might be taken away from among you. For I verily, as absent in body, but present in spirit, have judged already, as though I were present, concerning him that hath so done this deed, In the name of our Lord Jesus Christ, when ye are gathered together, and my spirit, with the power of our Lord Jesus Christ, To deliver such an one unto Satan for the destruction of the flesh, that the spirit may be saved in the day of the Lord Jesus. Your glorying is not good. Know ye not that a little leaven leaveneth the whole lump? Purge out therefore the old leaven, that ye may be a new lump, as ye are unleavened. For even Christ our passover is sacrificed for us: Therefore let us keep the feast, not with old leaven, neither with the leaven of malice and wickedness; but with the unleavened bread of sincerity and truth. I wrote unto you in an epistle not to company with fornicators: Yet not altogether with the fornicators of this world, or with the covetous, or extortioners, or with idolaters; for then must ye needs go out of the world. But now I have written unto you not to keep company, if any man that is called a brother be a fornicator, or covetous, or an idolater, or a railer, or a drunkard, or an extortioner; with such an one no not to eat. For what have I to do to judge them also that are without? do not ye judge them that are within? But them that are without God judgeth. Therefore put away from among yourselves that wicked person.—1 CORINTHIANS 5:1–13

This passage describes a sad situation in which a man in the church was living in gross immorality. Because the man was not repentant and was flaunting his sin, desiring to partake of the Lord's Table as if nothing was amiss, Paul instructed the church to let him go—to release him from the church's spiritual protection and membership.

Suppose this man had traveled to another city and attempted to partake of the Lord's Table in another church. If he were allowed, the other pastor would be unintentionally interfering with the Corinthian church's discipline.

God has given the ordinance of the Lord's Table as a sacred trust to His church. When before observing the Lord's Table we prepare and cleanse our hearts, God uses this special time to bring revival to the church.

To Ready for His Coming

For as often as ye eat this bread, and drink this cup, ye do shew the Lord's death till he come. —1 CORINTHIANS 11:26

Partaking of the Lord's Table focuses our attention back to the Cross, but it also points us forward to the Second Coming of Christ.

The Picture of His Coming

The first thing we see when we observe the Lord's Table is Christ's body that was broken and His blood that was shed. Next we look into our own hearts and examine ourselves, asking the Lord to reveal anything that is displeasing to Him. Then we are reminded of Christ's Second Coming in the phrase *"till he come."* Besides focusing our attention on Christ's death, the Lord's Table is a reminder of His return.

The Preparation for His Coming

The Lord's Table is a reminder to prepare for Christ's coming.

The first step in preparing for Christ's coming is to trust Him as your personal Saviour. Salvation is far weightier than partaking of the Lord's Table. Those who know Christ as Saviour can say with the Apostle Paul, *"...for I know whom I have believed, and am persuaded that he is able to keep that which I have committed unto him against that day"* (2 Timothy 1:12).

When we look back to the Cross, we are reminded of God's great love for us. The Bible teaches that God loves each of us and desires a genuine, personal relationship with us. John 3:16 says, *"For God so loved the world, that he gave his only begotten Son, that whosoever believeth in him should not perish, but have everlasting life."*

We must realize, however, that our sin separates us from God. The Bible says in Romans 3:23, *"For all have sinned, and come short of the glory of God."* And Romans 6:23 tells us that sin has a price that must be paid: *"For the wages* [payment] *of sin is death...."* The *death* referred to in this verse is eternal separation from God in a place called Hell (Revelation 20:14–15).

As we've already seen, Jesus bore the penalty of our sin when He shed His blood for us on the Cross. The payment for sin is death, *"But God commendeth* [proved] *his love toward us, in that, while we were yet sinners, Christ died for us"* (Romans 5:8). If you choose to receive Christ as your Saviour, you do not have to pay the price of death and Hell for your sin, because Jesus paid for our sins when He died on the Cross and rose again three days later!

If you have never trusted Christ, ask Him to be your Saviour, and claim His promise of eternal life. In Romans 10:13 the Bible says, *"For whosoever shall call upon the name of the Lord shall be saved."*

Far more important than partaking of the Lord's Table is being saved and prepared for Christ's return.

If you have already trusted Christ, realize that, as Christians, we prepare for Christ's coming by living in such a way that we could always anticipate His appearance with joy.

> *Behold, what manner of love the Father hath bestowed upon us, that we should be called the sons of God: therefore the world knoweth us not, because it knew him not. Beloved, now are we the sons of God, and it doth not yet appear what we shall be: but we know that, when he shall appear, we shall be like him; for we shall see him as he is. And every man that hath this hope in him purifieth himself, even as he is pure.*
> —1 John 3:1–3

If Christ should return right now, are you ready for His coming?

We've looked at three purposes for the Lord's Table. Primarily, it is given to us that we might remember the Lord and His sacrifice for us. The bread symbolizes His body—broken for us, and the cup symbolizes His blood—shed for us.

The Lord's Table also causes us to examine our own hearts for anything that would grieve the Lord. If the Lord has convicted you of sin, I implore you to confess it to the Lord and seek His forgiveness. Only when we are walking in fellowship with Him will we be ready for His coming.

The Ministry of a Deacon

The secret for the successful ministry of the early deacons is found in Acts 6:5. These men were *"full of faith and of the Holy Ghost."* These two elements are as vital for ministry today as they were in the first century.

We've explored some of the technical details of deacon ministry in this book, yet knowledge itself is insufficient to accomplish the work of God. A deacon with a thorough understanding of the operation of the church and complete faithfulness to assigned responsibility, but without faith or the Holy Spirit's power is spiritually fruitless. He may provide a measure of administrative assistance, but his ministry will lack fruit that remains for the glory of God (John 15:16).

Fruitful ministry requires that we abide in Christ. In John 15:4 Christ instructed His disciples (who would soon lead the first century church), *"Abide in me, and I in you. As the branch cannot bear fruit of itself, except it abide in the vine; no more can ye, except ye abide in me."*

Abiding in Christ includes spending time with Him regularly, filling our hearts and minds with Scripture, and yielding to the Holy Spirit's work in our own lives. These personal disciplines are the only way to a ministry that will have spiritual significance and eternal impact.

In Zechariah 4:6, God reminds us that what we accomplish for Him is, *"Not by might, nor by power, but by my spirit, saith the LORD of hosts."* When we serve in our own strength, we are limited by our finite resources. But deacons who are full of faith and of the Holy Spirit have the privilege of ministry that knows only the boundaries of the power of God.

PART THREE

Appendices

When I conducted my first deacons meeting as a young pastor, I had little idea of how to set in place policies that would direct our decisions. Through the years, our church has developed procedures, guidelines, and forms that have aided in the ministry. They have enabled us to serve with wise forethought and consistency. The following appendices are a compilation of some of these practices that have been helpful in our ministry.

Appendices 1–3 list our procedures for deacon nomination, annual deacons events, and the Lord's Table preparation. Appendix 4 provides descriptions of the deacon committees we have found helpful. Appendices 5–6 give our financial policies and procedures. Appendices 7–8 provide sample forms and a sample church constitution.

The Nomination of Deacons

A cts 6 outlines the selection of the first deacons of the church at Jerusalem. Several key phrases give us some insight as to how best to approach the nomination and election of deacons. Verse 3 says, "...*look ye out among you seven men of honest report, full of the Holy Ghost and wisdom, whom we may appoint over this business.*" This says that these were men who were from among the congregation and proven in their testimony.

At Lancaster Baptist Church, the deacons are the nominating committee, and each November they begin praying about potential new nominations for deacons. Members of the congregation may suggest names to the deacons at any time throughout the year.

At a deacons meeting in December, 3 x 5 cards are distributed on which each deacon may write down a few names for nomination. During the meeting, from those cards a master list is made by the pastor. At that point, each of the deacons have their heads bowed and eyes closed for a season of prayer. With heads remaining bowed and eyes closed, the pastor reads each of the names of those who have been nominated. If a deacon is aware of any situation in one of the nominees' life that would hinder him from becoming a deacon, he may raise his hand to indicate a veto of the nomination. This process allows for complete confidentiality and abstinence of gossip about any particular man.

Once this process is concluded, the pastor should have some names from which he can begin interviewing potential deacons. Each of these nominees has a meeting with the pastor. At the meeting, several items are shared with the nominee.

First, the nominee is congratulated for being unanimously nominated for the office of deacon. Then, the Bible is opened to 1 Timothy 3, where each of the qualifications of a pastor and deacon are defined. A complete list of deacon responsibilities is shared with the nominee as well as an approximate amount of time to be invested, should they accept the nomination. Items shared with the nominee at this time are the monthly deacons meetings, caring for widows, counting the offerings, attending Deacons Orientation, the responsibility for the wives to set up for the Lord's Table, and the need for deacons to serve the Lord's Table. Many other items may be shared at this time as well.

After the qualifications and job description of the deacon are shared, the nominee is given at least a week to pray about accepting the nomination. Should he determine to accept the nomination, his name is placed on a ballot for the annual Victory Meeting of Lancaster Baptist Church. The church family is instructed not to vote on "the best two out of three," but to vote on each individual who has been nominated. Traditionally, as these men are presented with the unanimous recommendation of the pastor and deacons, they have been elected to serve along side the other deacons of Lancaster Baptist Church. The term of service is two years, at which time they may be re-elected to serve an additional two years.

Annual Deacons Events

There are two very special annual events for the deacons and their wives that we host at Lancaster Baptist Church and highly recommend.

The first event is the annual Deacons Orientation. This retreat provides a time for the pastor to nurture and encourage the deacons in their family lives, deacon responsibilities, and overall commitments to the Lord Jesus Christ. Typically, this retreat takes place in a hotel setting, somewhere away from the church. The church budget allows for some offsetting of the cost of the retreat, with the deacons also contributing to the payment for the retreat.

Normally, we invite a guest speaker to bring the evening challenges, and the pastor speaks on issues ranging from benevolence and meeting the needs of widows to communicating during a building program. Split sessions may be offered to the deacons' wives where they learn more about serving with their husbands in the Deacon Ministry. Often, it is helpful to choose a deacon who has served for many years to speak on the subject of being an effective deacon.

This training has become invaluable over the years, and has helped to develop a cohesive team spirit amongst the deacons of Lancaster Baptist Church.

Another annual event that has been a tremendous blessing amongst the deacons is the Christmas party. This party is more than simply a time for food and fellowship. It is a time of reflection on the past year of victories and faithfulness of God. For many years, Terrie and I have purchased a gift for each deacon and his wife. We delight in the opportunity to thank them for being a blessing to our church family throughout the year.

Meetings like these are vitally important in the heart and life of a church. In leadership training sessions over the years, I have often said we need to spend "more time growing grass than killing weeds." The relationship development aspects of these types of retreats and parties will go a long way when challenges come into the life of a church.

Lord's Table Preparation and Procedures

The Lord's Table is a sacred time and should be treated with the right spirit. The deacons' wives who help to set up the Lord's Table should have their hearts prepared, not only when partaking, but also during the time of preparation. This should be accomplished decently and in order (1 Corinthians 14:33, 40).

The outline below is the preparation procedures our deacons' wives follow as they set up and clean up for the Lord's Table. A schedule for which ladies are involved for each service is distributed at the Deacons Orientation in February.

A. Double check the schedule and know when you are scheduled for setup or cleanup.

   1. Each team is made up of deacons' wives and is scheduled for three setups, three cleanups, and six off-months per year. Make sure to plan accordingly.

2. Each team has a team leader to help in reminding her team when they are scheduled.

B. This is a sacred time and should be accomplished in the right heart and spirit. Have a place for your children. They should not be in the setup room or helping with the Lord's Table.

C. Lord's Table setup should be accomplished in the proper place. Choose an appropriate, quiet, and private room.

D. Any out-of-the-ordinary circumstances will be communicated from the deacon to the setup team. Examples would be: services in which a greater attendance is expected or if extra juice is needed in certain areas of the auditorium.

E. Be sure to contact the supply team leader if supplies are getting low so more supplies can be ordered.

Committee Descriptions

Lancaster Baptist Church does not officially have functioning committees for the purpose of ministry operations. However, the deacons do formulate select committees to serve the congregation and the pastor more effectively in developing the ministries and membership of the church. These committees are not a separate office but are created by the pastor based on perceived ministry needs.

Committees are changed, and members are re-assigned from time to time. Some deacons serve on multiple committees. The pastor is a de facto member of all committees.

Listed below is a brief description of the committees presently formed by the deacons of our church:

Building, Safety and Expansion Committee

Members of this committee will attend building committee meetings during pre-construction and construction times. If they are unable to attend the weekday meetings, they will receive meeting minutes and coordinate with the chairman and staff coordinator. They may be asked to make phone calls and assist in research during the project. They will be apprised of budget changes or construction changes throughout the project.

Legal Committee

This committee will be responsible for keeping notes for all meetings. They will attend CLA seminars as available. They will be apprised of any potential pending legal issues with the church prior to the upcoming deacons meeting. They will have a working knowledge of church constitution and policies manual and staff.

Missions Committee

Members of this committee will review monthly missions correspondence, help develop and maintain missionary classifications with the Senior Pastor and Missions Director of the church. They will apprise the pastor of any missionary needs.

School Committee

This committee will review the annual budget with the Finance Director prior to the presentation of the budget. They will review any potential scholarship monies and help assess the need of distribution. They will assist with any major discipline issues or financial issues within the school community.

College Committee

This committee will work with the college vice presidents on an as needed basis for contacting potential donors. They will coordinate with the college administration regarding graduation exercises or any special events during which the college and deacon body interface.

Lord's Table Committee

This committee will be responsible for communicating with the deacons' wives regarding setup and cleanup for the Lord's Table. The chairman will provide a schedule for the distribution of the Lord's Table. This would include having Pastoral Staff members fill in should a deacon be absent or additional help needed in distributing the Lord's Table.

Discipline Committee

This committee will help in the spirit of Matthew 18 and Galatians 6 to confront members who are living lives that are sinful and harmful to the body of Lancaster Baptist Church. This will be coordinated with the Pastoral Staff on an as needed basis.

Finance Committee

This committee will work with the Senior Pastor and Financial Administrator at the pastor's discretion. They will develop the count schedule and update counting policies and procedures. They will also meet with the Financial Administrator prior to the monthly deacons meeting to review reconciliations and understand the report to be presented at the deacons meeting. Their concern should be the budget process and progress.

Audit Committee

This committee will work with the Senior Pastor and Financial Administrator according to the policy. They will help in choosing and approving the church auditor on an annual basis. They will also meet with the Financial Administrator to review the audit report and present it at the following deacons meeting. Their concern should be to assess the product of our internal control system.

Compensation Committee

This committee will work with the Senior Pastor in the establishment of annual raises and bonuses for the leadership team members of

Lancaster Baptist Church. The policies and minutes of meetings will be kept in a locked file in the pastor's office and the annual adjustments will be delivered to the payroll department directly. This committee will work together as a team to make recommendations for the Senior Pastor's compensation and will make the information regarding increased percentages or bonuses available to the deacon body. All studies, documentation, and recommendations shall be filed in the compensation committee files.

All committees that conduct meetings during the month turn in their meeting minutes to the legal committee for entrance into the official record of the deacons of Lancaster Baptist Church.

Financial Policies and Offering Count Procedures

A commonly questioned area amongst growing churches in America today is the area of financial management within the context of the local church.

Perhaps the first realm of questioning revolves around the area of accountability. Lancaster Baptist Church is a church that has worked diligently to maintain financial integrity. We have felt this to be especially necessary, since we have been involved in constant building programs, due to the growth of the church.

Annual Audits & Reviews

In order to maintain proper checks and balances, Lancaster Baptist Church has had financial audits and reviews done on an annual basis for many years. We have chosen a certified public accounting firm who audits or reviews the books of Lancaster Baptist Church and ministries, and these audits have always been available for membership review upon request.

Financial Policy to New Members

Each new member of Lancaster Baptist Church receives a copy of our financial policy in his new member's packet. Amongst other things the policy says, "We will provide an annual report to our church members and welcome questions throughout the year." We believe that one of the healthy signs of a church is that the leadership remains approachable to these types of questions. We truly invite questions from the earliest moments of one's membership, and we are thankful for the great level of involvement, questions, and support we have received from our members over the years.

Training Seminars

Through the years, Lancaster Baptist Church has developed a very extensive policies manual for the church employees. Many of these policies relate to the handling of finances and reflect the years of training and seminars our staff has attended at conferences sponsored by groups, such as the Christian Law Association and the National Association of Church Business Administration.

Several years ago, sensing the growth of the ministry, we prayerfully added to our staff a financial administrator, whose background in finance and degree in business administration brought additional and helpful systems to our ministry.

Over the past several years, we have received valuable input from the Christian Law Association as well as other consultants. These outside firms, combined with the daily oversight of our church bookkeepers and financial administrator have helped to maintain the Lord's testimony here at Lancaster Baptist Church. Also, the monthly review by our church deacons of the church accounts has provided for the highest levels of accountability and financial integrity on behalf of our church family. The deacons ask questions and make suggestions in every meeting. It is inconceivable to me that the entire deacon board would see anything lacking integrity, and fail to speak. Only God knows the heart of someone who would suggest otherwise. Again, members with a question or concern are encouraged to view the books of Lancaster Baptist Church.

Fair & Reasonable Compensation

We have also endeavored to be vigilant in the area of compensating our church staff in accordance with nationally known pay scales. We have conducted surveys of various churches and Christian ministries, similar to ours, in scope and size. Additionally, the National Association of Church Business Administration annually conducts a national church survey of compensation. This survey provides ranges of compensation for each position within the local church. This study is evaluated by our deacons and pastoral staff in the development of the church budget.

Sometimes folks who question areas in this realm are comparing what they have seen in a much smaller church environment to this particular church ministry environment. The level of leadership, amount of pressure and overall scope of ministry that is required on the staff of a church with several thousand active members, demands that we are consistent and competitive in our care for godly staff members whose labor is worthy of their hire.

On a personal level, Terrie and I have tried to be wise and Christ-honoring stewards. We have tried to invest wisely, and have given, sacrificially, over the years. We have never asked our church family to do what we have not done.

Pastors are people who have families and family needs like anyone else. Terrie and I have been blessed by God and we are thankful.

My opinion in these areas is that these are personal issues and, when someone raises questions about these issues, they are dealing, mainly, with their personal preference. Finally, I would say that someone may disagree with the way a pastor dresses, the investments he makes, the home in which he lives, or the salary the deacons select for him. These are often matters of personal opinion and interpretation.

Offering Count Procedures

Pastors often request a copy of the offering count procedures we follow here at Lancaster Baptist Church. Our counting procedures are in accordance with the Policies Manual of the church. These policies maintain the integrity of the financial dealings of the church and are in accordance with legal counsel from the Christian Law Association, as well as our certified public accountants.

The counting of the offering is to be done in confidentiality and is not to be discussed with anyone. Deacons are scheduled on a rotating basis to count the offering.

A. POLICY

It is the policy of the Lancaster Baptist Church that all offerings shall be counted and deposited in their entirety in the appropriate ministry accounts within twenty-four hours of receipt or collection. Exceptions to this policy may be made by the Senior Pastor for special offerings, e.g., Missions Conference, etc., in which case the offering will be secured in the safe in accordance with this procedure. The counting of the offering is to be done in confidentiality and not to be discussed with anyone. There shall be no withholding of cash from incoming cash receipts to cover current or past due ministry expenses, savings for future expenditures, payroll, bonuses, gifts, love offerings, travel expenses, expense reimbursements, cash advances, or any other unapproved cash need. A copy of this procedure will be maintained in the count room for reference purposes. *(See sample Count Team Task Breakdown form and the Currency Breakdown form in Appendix 7.)*

B. **GENERAL GUIDELINES FOR HANDLING OFFERINGS**

1. Offering defined—offerings are monies in the form of checks, coinage, currency, money orders, debit or credit card receipts or tangible property of value which are given for use in the ministries of Lancaster Baptist Church.

2. All offerings will be in the control of no less than two approved people at all times unless in a locked safe or in a dual-controlled, sealed bank deposit bag.

3. Only approved ushers are allowed to collect the offerings. West Coast Baptist College students may be used as ushers for special occasions, e.g., Leadership Conference, upon approval by the Head Usher and Senior Pastor. Appropriate training will be provided by the Head Usher as needed.

4. Deacons are the approved counters for church offerings.

5. Safe locations, safe combinations, offering collection, counting, and depositing procedures are confidential and shall not be disclosed to any individual unless authorized by the Senior Pastor or Financial Administrator.

6. Information which could jeopardize the security and/ or integrity of the offering handling process should be immediately communicated to the Senior Pastor or Financial Administrator.

7. A drop safe located in the Worship Center Information Center shall be used to secure any offering which cannot be processed in accordance with these guidelines. Offerings

placed in the drop safe are removed at least weekly by the Financial Administrator and secured in the count room.

8. Deacons shall not write personal checks for cash and/ or exchange currency for other denominations during the count.

9. The Spanish offering totals will be separately noted prior to being merged into the general offering deposit.

Detailed count procedures

A. RESPONSIBILITIES

Each count team member is responsible for adherence to LBC offering count procedures and for maintaining the integrity and confidentiality of the count process. Offerings should never be left unattended and shall be supervised by at least two deacons at all times. Supervision shall consist of a direct and constant visual accounting of the offering.

B. COUNT ROOM

Counting of offerings is to be conducted in the count room. Special offerings may be counted in an alternate secure location only upon prior approval of the Senior Pastor.

The count room door is to remain locked and secure at all times. If an important purpose exists, entry and exit of the count room during the count process shall be conducted with verbal notice to the count team members and in a careful and timely manner. At no time shall an unauthorized person enter the count room. The digital code to unlock the count room door is privileged information and shall not be divulged without express authorization from the Senior Pastor or member of the pastoral leadership team. Any breach of this code shall be immediately reported to a member of the pastoral leadership team.

No jackets, coats, books, Bibles or food items are allowed inside the count room. Coat hooks and book shelves are provided to secure these items in the vestibule just adjacent to the count room. Beverages such as bottled water, canned soda or coffee are allowed, however, such items shall be consumed so as not to impede or compromise the integrity of the count process.

C. COUNT TEAM

1. Deacons of LBC will comprise members of the count team. New deacons will observe two counts before being assigned duties as an active count team member.

2. A count team shall consist of at least four deacons. If four deacons are not available, the offering shall remain secured in the count room safe until such time as a proper count team can be comprised. The Finance Administrator will be notified of this occurrence. Count responsibilities are to take priority over other ministry duties which may delay the count, e.g., meetings.

3. No deacons who are related by blood or marriage shall be on the same count team.

4. One deacon shall be designated as the Lead Counter (designated as LC) for the team. The Lead Counter will be responsible for overseeing the counting of the offering and will observe all aspects of the count process. The Lead Counter will verify the count totals and sign on the Currency Breakdown Worksheet (Exhibit A) under Lead Counter Verification and initial the deposit slip prepared by the Check Processor (refer to #5 below as "CC").

5. Additional positions to be designated in the monthly Counting Schedule are:

    •   Checks/Calculator (designated as CC)—this position, also referred to as "Check Processor" is responsible for receiving checks from count team members as they are separated from the cash offering and totaling the checks using a tape calculator. Checks will be totaled and bundled in batches of approximately 50 checks. Each bundled total will be noted on a deposit slip, to be verified by the Checks/Calculator person and the Lead Counter.

- Cash/Coin Machine (designated as CM)—this person will count all coin in the offering by using the coin counting machine provided in the count room. Separate totals may be required, depending upon the offering, e.g., March Building Offering.
- Cash/Coin Verifier (designated as CV)—this position will count all currency using the currency counting machine provided in the count room. Generally, batches of 100 will be counted unless lower numbers remain or are dictated by the offering. Bundles of same monetary designation, e.g., $1, $5, $10, $20, etc. will be created using bank straps provided in the count room.
- Spanish Count (designated as SC)—this position will count the Spanish offering, compile a total amount using a tape calculator. This total is to be used internally within LBC. The Spanish offering will then be merged with the general offering total.

6. The Lead Counter will be responsible for overseeing the counting of the offering and will observe all aspects of the count process and shall sign all forms and deposit slips verifying the total amount of the offering and deposit.

7. Deacons will be assigned to a count team on a monthly basis by the Count Team Scheduler. The Lead Counter will be designated on the monthly schedule. Deacons who are assigned to a count schedule and are unable to participate in the count are responsible for seeking a replacement as

promptly as is reasonably practicable. The absent deacon shall notify at least one of the count team members of their anticipated absence whenever possible.

8. General Count Team Members will be responsible for being familiar with and performing count functions in compliance with the following detailed procedures.

Specific tasks

A. Retrieving offerings from safe

1. Sunday morning, Sunday evening, and Wednesday evening offerings will be secured inside one of the safes.

2. The safes are monitored by a video surveillance camera.

3. To insure accountability for offerings, two deacons must be present whenever the safe is opened. One deacon opening the safe must use his fingerprint and PIN code to open the safe. A second deacon will use an assigned key to open the padlock on the safe.

4. A logbook shall be maintained inside the safe and shall be used to document all safe access. A log book entry shall be made each time the safe is opened, noting the date, time, purpose and individuals accessing the safe. Two separate deacons' signatures must be entered in the log book for each access to the safe.

5. All offerings shall be secured inside the safe in a locked box or bag. This box or bag shall be removed from the safe and transported by two deacons in its locked state to the count room.

6. Once securely inside the count room, the locked box or bag will be opened at the direction of the Lead Counter.

7. Confirmation of the presence of a Spanish offering will be conducted upon removal of the offering from the safe to insure a Spanish offering is included. If not, the

transporting deacons will notify the Lead Counter. Attempts may be made to locate the Spanish offering. Attempts with negative results shall result in notification of Financial Administrator at the earliest reasonable opportunity. The absence of a Spanish offering will not delay commencement of the count process. If the Spanish offering cannot be located in sufficient time to be included in the respective offering count, then that Spanish offering shall be secured in the safe to be counted the next day by the Financial Administrator and deposited in the bank. At no time should an offering remain in any safe for more than twenty-four hours.

B. **Retrieving offerings from count room safe**

1. Offerings counted from the Sunday morning services will be secured inside the count room safe.
2. The count room and its safe shall be monitored by video surveillance camera.
3. All procedures described above for access to the Foyer safe will be utilized to access the count room safe.

C. **Counting cash, coins, checks**

1. The entire count process will be observed by the Lead Counter. The Lead Counter shall be positioned with calculator at the head of the table nearest the door. Upon completion of the count sheet and deposit slip, count team processors will sign and forward each document, along with the filled, but unsealed, deposit bag to the Lead Counter for verification of each entry and calculation. The accuracy of the calculations on the deposit slip and count sheet will be independently verified by the Lead Counter using a calculator. The Lead Counter will then sign the count sheet and deposit slip, insert copies in the deposit

bag and seal the bag. The deposit bag will then be secured in the count room safe for deposit by LBC Security staff.

2. The Spanish offering will be counted and totaled separately from the general offering. Once the Spanish offering has been totaled, that figure will be noted and then merged with the general offering.

3. Offering envelopes will be separated from the loose coins and currency.

4. Loose coins shall be placed inside a canvas bag and secured in the count room safe. Coins will be counted weekly by the 4 PM count team designee. A coin counter provided by LBC shall be used for coin counting. A separate deposit slip for the weekly coin offering will be prepared by the 4 PM count team designee, and approved by the Lead Counter. The totaled coin offering will be secured in the count room safe, where it will be later removed by LBC Security staff with the general offering deposit.

5. Loose currency shall be placed into a plastic bin in the middle of the count table.

6. Cash counting will be conducted by counters not involved with processing checks.

7. An electronic cash counting machine will be used to count stacks of 100 bills, each in separate denominations of $1, $5, $10, $20, $50, and $100. The machine shall be located in the center of the count table. All stacks of 100 bills will be paper strapped and clearly identified by denomination.

8. Two counters will verify that the proper count has been achieved for each stack of currency. All currency shall be run through the counter successfully without mishap a minimum of two times to confirm the stack contains 100 bills of the same denomination. The two counters shall sign the cash sheet verifying the total cash amount

(Exhibit A) This total will be included on the deposit slip (Exhibit B).

9. Counters shall rotate cash counting machine duties weekly.
10. Offering envelopes are prepared for checks coming in without an envelope.
11. For envelopes where the name may be illegible, the counter may rewrite the name on the envelope based on the name on the enclosed check.
12. Contents of envelopes are verified to the outside of the envelope. If there is a difference, the correct amount is written on the envelope and initialed by the counter making the correction and verified and initialed by a second counter.
13. The method of giving is noted on the outside of the envelope (e.g., Cash, CK (check), MO (money order), etc.).
14. The name and address on a check will be written on the envelope in cases where the check does not match the name on the giving envelope.
15. Using a 10-key calculator, two tapes are run on the checks. The tapes must agree before the count is considered ready for deposit.
16. The back of all checks are stamped with the church's "FOR DEPOSIT ONLY" endorsement stamp for the church's bank account.
17. Using the calculator, two tapes are run on the currency. The tapes must agree before the count is considered ready for deposit.
18. A Currency Breakdown Worksheet is prepared that lists the number and amount of checks deposited and lists by denomination the currency deposited (e.g., $100s–$2,100; $50s–$500; etc.). The Worksheet will be signed by the

Cash/Coin Verifier, Cash/Coin Counter, Check Processor and Lead Counter.

19. A deposit slip shall be prepared by the Check Processor for the bank that lists the amount of checks by batches of 25–50 and lists by total amount the currency deposited. The Check Processor will indicate the date of service, the deposit bag number and sign under "Prepared by." The completed and signed original deposit slip as well as the original Currency Breakdown Worksheet will be stapled together and be included in the deposit bag which will be placed in the safe for transport to the bank at the designated time.

20. A copy of the deposit slip and Currency Breakdown Worksheet together with the verified envelopes shall be placed in a secure place for pickup by the Church Bookkeeper.

21. Non-cash items are to be tagged and noted on a giving envelope and secured in the count room safe for removal by the Financial Administrator. The envelope will be routed to the Financial Administrator with the other envelopes.

22. The deposit is placed into a disposable security deposit bag and the seal is detached from the bag and stapled to the Deposit Sheet that will go to the Church Bookkeeper.

23. The sealed deposit bag will be secured inside the count room safe.

24. The bank deposit of the Wednesday offering will be conducted by LBC Security staff on Thursday mornings.

25. The bank deposit of the Sunday offerings will be conducted by LBC Security staff on Monday mornings.

Guidelines for Helping the Needy

On a rotating basis, the deacons stand in the lobby after the church services to assist the pastor with needs of the church family, as those asking for financial assistance. An application (included in Appendix 7) should be given to those requesting assistance, and the need assessed upon the return of the completed application at a future church service or by a selected pastoral staff member in the church office.

It is important to remember that every person's problem is a crisis to him or her. Whether or not the situation is worthy, people asking for help should be treated with kindness and respect that would honor the Lord. The guidelines that follow will allow the deacon to be kind but deliberate when dealing with someone who is demanding, engaged in sin, or uncooperative.

The procedures we follow at Lancaster Baptist Church in helping the needy differ somewhat for those who are members of the church and those who are not. We designate a portion of our monthly budget for benevolence, and we give priority to our members.

Those Who Are Members of the Church

As we have therefore opportunity, let us do good unto all men, especially unto them who are of the household of faith.—GALATIANS 6:10

From time to time there are members who are going to request financial assistance from the church. Such requests are factored into the budget annually; however, great discernment must be used with the distribution of funds or help for the church family.

Who should be helped?
- Be responsible stewards with the amount of budgeted funds for the needy within and without the church. First Corinthians 4:2 says, *"Moreover it is required in stewards, that a man be found faithful."* Remember to help as many people as possible rather than distributing funds to a "select few."
- Analyze whether or not the financial need is due to poor financial management on the part of the member. A session on budgeting may be required with one of the men of the church prior to helping the member financially.
- Do not create a dependency on the church for a prolonged period, especially to those who are not actively seeking employment. The church is not a social or government agency, and though people should be treated with love and sensitivity, they, not the church, are responsible for the consequences of their decisions. Second Thessalonians 3:10 says, *"For even when we were with you, this we commanded you, that if any would not work, neither should he eat."*

- The goal is to seek to help each member learn to depend on the Lord and have a mind to work. Philippians 4:5–7 says, *"Let your moderation be known unto all men. The Lord is at hand. Be careful for nothing; but in every thing by prayer and supplication with thanksgiving let your requests be made known unto God. And the peace of God, which passeth all understanding, shall keep your hearts and minds through Christ Jesus."*
- Remember that those who are helped the most will often resent you at a later time for the help. In the long run, they will appreciate your prayer and godly counsel more than financial help. A child who is continuously "bailed out" by his parents will never truly learn how to provide for himself and will ultimately lose respect for his parents.
- Active members take first priority. If a family who has faithfully supported the local church "hits hard times," they are not only a part of "God's family," but they are truly a part of the "Household of Faith" locally. Inactive members often come to the church only in time of need, and we must not foster and promote their crisis mentality.
- Widows also should be treated with high priority and respect. Acts 6 implies that the early church ministered very conscientiously to the widows. Any need of a widow should be handled quickly and efficiently (see 1 Timothy 5:3–10).
- Single mothers who have been abandoned by their husbands must also be considered as a priority.

Guidelines for assistance:
- If the need is highly confidential or personally sensitive, it will be dealt with by the pastoral staff.
- If a member calls the pastor, and it is determined that a deacon can help, a deacon will be assigned as a temporary "case worker." The deacon's ministry, in this capacity, should not be prolonged for more than one month without

the pastor's knowledge, and his involvement should be reported on the Monthly Deacon Report Form.

- We do not pay for credit card bills or cable/satellite television bills.
- We can help with housing and basic utility needs.
- We may also help with car needs.
- We do not give cash or checks made out to an individual. Checks will be written to the company involved, whether it be a utility company, car repair, etc.
- Any amount over $100 should be cleared through the pastor without the member's knowledge.
- Food assistance is given in the form of gift cards to a local grocery store. Through an arrangement with the grocery store, the gift cards we purchase cannot be used for alcohol, tobacco or lottery tickets.
- An assistance log is maintained in the Information Center. The log must be checked before assistance is promised so that disbursements are not duplicated, and so that assistance is not given too frequently.

Those Who are Non-Members or Travelers through the Area

The following are guidelines that should be used when assisting people who are destitute or needy and have no affiliation with the church:

- Remember that, while these people have had difficult situations with their finances, they still are souls for whom Jesus Christ shed His blood. Never give any assistance to such people without sharing with them the Gospel of Christ. Sometimes people will say a prayer in hope of receiving assistance. While this decision may not be for

Christ, we must not judge a person's motive
left between the individual and the Lord H
our responsibility to save souls. It is our respoɩ₁ɔ.
preach the Word.

- Godly discernment and efficient administration are vital in these situations in order to not only properly steward our resources, but also to prevent establishing a reputation that would draw in transients seeking to take advantage of the church's generosity. Those seeking assistance will be asked to sign an agreement of their understanding and compliance to our requirements before their request is reviewed.
- We will require positive IDs of each member in the household or group traveling together, including children. Proof of marriage must be shown for those claiming to be husband and wife with IDs in different names.
- We will require proof of ownership and registration of any vehicle being driven.
- We will require a name and telephone number of someone we can (and will) contact to confirm the traveler's situation.
- We will not provide cash.
- We will not provide lodging to single individuals or unmarried couples.
- We reserve the right to check police records and cooperate with the authorities on any ongoing criminal investigation.
- Single mothers and children should receive our attention and help in a priority sequence over an able-bodied man.
- Persons who indulge in habits such as smoking, drinking, and drugs may receive limited food items or help with utility bills. However, we will not provide continual care for those who deny the biblical principles of stewardship in their everyday lives.

- Food items or utility bill assistance of over $75 will not be provided for those couples who are living outside of wedlock. In dealing with such families, the plan of approach would be:

  a) Help them with their initial need. Set up a time of counseling with a deacon at which time salvation will be presented, and then steps for recovery can be presented. In some cases this may mean that couples should be married if they intend to live together. Any couple who will follow the biblical steps to recovering spiritually and financially will qualify for continual help. In essence, anyone who comes to our church may receive limited help the first time. However, no one will be continually helped who is living in violation of Scripture.

  b) Able-bodied men may also be helped with limited food items and other physical needs. We do not give cash assistance, nor can we allow non-members to work for money or food. This could present a potential insurance liability problem.

- No transient individual or family shall be housed on the church property. Also, no family shall be recommended to live with a church family unless they have frequented the church services often enough to receive pastoral approval in this matter. Families may receive one night of lodging assistance from our church (in certain cases, up to three nights). One night of lodging assistance does not require the pastor's approval.

- The deacons of the church shall be notified by ushers and, at times, pastoral staff members regarding the needs of visitors such as are herein described. Also, deacons should be sensitive toward the pastor after each service to help in the event that he is being "cornered" or "pressured" by anyone for assistance. Kind, gentle, loving, and firm intervention should take place on the part of the pastoral staff or the deacons in the event of such an occurrence. This does not imply that the pastor has no sensitivity toward those in need; however, after the services, the pastor is greeting the flock and dealing with people. At times, there may be certain security risks involved with those who perhaps feel they did not get as much help as they needed. Deacons should exercise caution and plan for the unexpected.

- In the event the person seeking assistance is obviously under the influence of alcohol or drugs, two deacons should work in these particular cases. A deacon should not leave the pastor or another deacon alone with anyone of questionable manner.
- In the event that a woman is the sole requester of assistance, a deacon and deacon's wife, or in the case a wife is not available, two deacons, to deal with this situation.

The guidelines that have been given are in no way all-conclusive; however, they should provide a more specific direction as we continue to minister in the twenty-first century. We must always remember to have love and compassion on those in their times of need. We must always remember that our Saviour came "not to be ministered unto, but to minister." Certainly it would be a shame for any servant of God to feel that he or she is above helping the needy. This would be a sign of carnality and something that is not pleasing to the Saviour. The pastor and pastoral staff deal daily with these types of needs; however, our deacons will help fulfill this role in and around service times to allow the pastoral staff to more effectively lead, direct, and guide the overall flock of the church. Special situations and questions may be directed to the pastor during the regular meetings or at other times, should a need be of an urgent nature.

Sample Forms

Decision Card

(Fill out **completely** and return to the **Information Center**)

Date: _____ (Please print in black or blue ink)

Name: _____

Address: _____

City: _____ State: _____ Zip Code: _____

Phone: _____ Email: _____

LifeStage:

❑ Single ❑ Married ❑ Widow(er) ❑ Other _____

Age: _____ Birthday: _____ Anniversary: _____

Decision:

❑ Salvation ❑ Baptism ❑ Assurance ❑ Other: _____

Counselor: _____

Lancaster Baptist Church | 4020 E. Lancaster Blvd. | Lancaster, CA 93535
661.946.4663 | lancasterbaptist.org | Paul Chappell, Pastor

My Personal Testimony

"Then they that gladly received his word were baptized: and the same day there were added unto them about three thousand souls." Acts 2:41

When I Accepted Christ
When and how did you receive Jesus Christ as your personal Saviour?

_____
_____
_____
_____
_____
_____
_____
_____
_____
_____
_____
_____

When and Where I Was Baptized
Have you been baptized in a Baptist church?_____

If so, do you remember when and where? _____
_____

If you have not been baptized in a Baptist Church are you willing to identify with this church body in water baptism?

_____
_____

"For the perfecting of the saints, for the work of the ministry, for the edifying of the body of Christ: Till we all come in the unity of the faith, and of the knowledge of the Son of God, unto a perfect man, unto the measure of the stature of the fulness of Christ:"—Ephesians 4:12—13

(Please be sure to complete the back of this form.)

Membership Transfer

Adult Membership:

Date:_____

Mr. / Miss / Mrs. _____

StreetAddress:_____Apt.#_____

MailingAddress:_____

City:_____

State:_____ Zip:_____

Phone#_____

Email: _____

PresentChurchMembership:_____

_____

Address:_____

City:_____State:_____Zip:_____

Birthday:(His)_____(Hers)_____

Anniversary:_____

Marital Status:

☐ Single   ☐ Married   ☐ Widowed   ☐ Other:_____

Children's Membership:

Children under the age of 18, who have been saved and baptized in a Baptist church, will receive membership at the same time as their parent/legal guardian. Children who have not yet received Christ as Saviour will become members when they are saved and then baptized. Please list the names of all children and indicate whether or not they have been saved and baptized in a Baptist church.

_____ Birthday:_____	☐ Saved ☐ Baptized
_____ Birthday:_____	☐ Saved ☐ Baptized
_____ Birthday:_____	☐ Saved ☐ Baptized
_____ Birthday:_____	☐ Saved ☐ Baptized

Counselor's Name:_____

NOTE: Membership is finalized upon receipt of records from your former church.

Application for Assistance
Lancaster Baptist Church Benevolence Program

In order to request assistance from the Lancaster Baptist Church benevolence program, this application and a financial profile must be filled out in its entirety. This is a confidential application for review by the Benevolence Committee only. Additional information may be required to make an appropriate decision.

Please Print

Today's Date: _____ Date Assistance Needed: _____

Applicant's Name: _____ SSN: _____

Spouse's Name: _____ Marital Status: _____

Home Address: _____ City, State, Zip: _____

Phone (day): _____ Phone (evening): _____

Driver's State: _____ License Number: _____ Date of Birth: _____

Please list the names and ages of children currently living in your household.

_____	_____	_____
(Name)	(Age)	(Relation to Child)
_____	_____	_____
(Name)	(Age)	(Relation to Child)
_____	_____	_____
(Name)	(Age)	(Relation to Child)
_____	_____	_____
(Name)	(Age)	(Relation to Child)
_____	_____	_____
(Name)	(Age)	(Relation to Child)
_____	_____	_____
(Name)	(Age)	(Relation to Child)

How long have you lived at your address? _____ Do you ____ own ____ rent

Vehicle 1   Make: _____ Model: _____
            Year: _____ License Number: _____ State: _____

Vehicle 2   Make: _____ Model: _____
            Year: _____ License Number: _____ State: _____

Do you _____ own _____ lease

Are you a member of Lancaster Baptist Church? _____ How long? _____

Are you a member of an Adult Bible Class? _____ Which one? _____

What past or present ministries have you served in at Lancaster Baptist Church?
_____

Where does your closest relative live? _____
Does he/she know about your need? _____

Are you receiving assistance from any other source (examples: family, unemployment, other churches, etc.)? _____
If so, please list source of assistance and amount/type of assistance received.
_____

Current Employer   Name: _____ Phone: _____
                   Address: _____
Spouse's Employer Name: _____ Phone: _____
                   Address: _____

If unemployed, please list when and where you were last employed.
Date of Termination: _____
Name: _____ Phone: _____
Address: _____

What other resources offered at Lancaster Baptist Church have you pursued (example: pastoral counseling, financial classes, reformer's unanimous)?
_____

Have you applied or received assistance from Lancaster Baptist Church in the past? _____
If yes, what was the amount of assistance? _____

Have you (and your spouse, if married) received any financial counseling in the past? _____

If we offer assistance, you may be required to participate in a financial program at Lancaster Baptist Church consisting of multiple sessions. Are you willing to make this commitment? _____

TOTAL AMOUNT REQUESTED: $_____ (required)

Please state a summary of your need(s): _____
_____
_____
_____

What event(s) has occurred that has prompted your need for assistance? _____
_____
_____
_____

Please prioritize your need(s):

_____ _____ _____ _____
(Description of Expense) (Purpose) (Payable To) (Amount)

_____ _____ _____ _____
(Description of Expense) (Purpose) (Payable To) (Amount)

_____ _____ _____ _____
(Description of Expense) (Purpose) (Payable To) (Amount)

_____ _____ _____ _____
(Description of Expense) (Purpose) (Payable To) (Amount)

_____ _____ _____ _____
(Description of Expense) (Purpose) (Payable To) (Amount)

_____ _____ _____ _____
(Description of Expense) (Purpose) (Payable To) (Amount)

We require positive IDs of each member in the household or group traveling together, including children.
We require proof of marriage for those claiming to be husband and wife with IDs in different names.
We require proof of ownership and registration of any vehicle being driven.
We require a name and telephone number of someone we can (and do) contact to confirm your situation.
We do not provide cash.
We do not provide lodging to single individuals or unmarried couples.
We reserve the right to check police records.
We will cooperate with the authorities in any ongoing criminal investigation.

I, the undersigned, certify that to the best of my knowledge the information listed on this form is true and accurate, and that I understand and will cooperate with the above requirements.

Signature: _____ Date: _____

For Office Use Only

Approved? _____ Yes _____ No

Assistance Provided: _____

_____

Signature of Deacon: _____ Date: _____

Signature of Administration: _____ Date: _____

Deacon's Monthly Report Sheet

Name: _____   **Date:** _____

         Name: **Response:**

I.   New member packets delivered:

_____
_____
_____

II.   Meals delivered:

_____
_____
_____

III. Visits on elderly:

_____
_____
_____

IV. Cards sent:

_____
_____
_____

V.   Fellowship you initiated:

_____
_____
_____

VI. Other areas of service:

_____
_____
_____

* Please fill out each month and bring to monthly deacons meeting.

Lancaster Baptist Church · 4020 E. Lancaster Blvd. · Lancaster, CA 93535
661.946.4663 · lancasterbaptist.org · Paul Chappell, Pastor

COUNT TEAM TASK BREAKDOWN

Exhibit C

Date: _____

Check appropriate service:

Early Sunday Count _____
Late Sunday Count _____
Wednesday Count _____
Other _____

Deacon Print Name	Deacon Signature	CHECK BOX FOR EVERY DUTY PERFORMED						
		Lead Counter	Verify Envelopes & Sorting		Currency	Deposit Slip		
			Checks	Currency	Counter	Total Checks	Endorse Checks	

Currency Breakdown Worksheet

DATE: _____

Cash:	Amount
$ 1.00 x _____ =	
$ 2.00 x _____ =	
$ 5.00 x _____ =	
$ 10.00 x _____ =	
$ 20.00 x _____ =	
$ 50.00 x _____ =	
$100.00 x _____ =	

Total Cash $ _____

Total Coin $ _____

Total Checks $ _____

Total Deposit $_____

Currency Counted by: _____
(Signature & Printed Name)

Currency Verified by: _____
(Signature & Printed Name)

Checks Processed by: _____
(Signature & Printed Name)

Lead Counter Approval: _____
(Signature & Printed Name)

Sample Church Constitution

The following is the constitution used by our church. From time to time we have updated our constitution to reflect new procedures or address current issues.

ARTICLE 1—NAME AND PURPOSE

SECTION 1.01—NAME

This corporation, congregation of believers, shall be known as Lancaster Baptist Church.

Lancaster Baptist Temple of Antelope Valley's articles of incorporation were officially approved February 17, 1976. The constitution and bylaws were amended June 28, 1995 to include the change of the name of the corporation to Lancaster Baptist Church. The constitution and bylaws were revised May 4, 2005.

SECTION 1.02—PURPOSE

(A) This congregation is organized as a church exclusively for charitable, religious, and educational purposes within the meaning of Section 501 (c) (3) of the Internal Revenue Code of 1986 (or the corresponding provision of any future United States Revenue Law), including, but not limited to, for such purposes, the establishing and maintaining of religious worship, the building of churches, parsonages, schools, colleges, chapels, radio stations, television stations, rescue missions, print shops, daycare centers, camps, nursing homes, and cemeteries, and any other ministries that the pastor may be led of God to establish in the United States and in any foreign country.

(B) The purpose and mission of this church shall be to labor by the help of God, and the power of the Holy Spirit, to carry out the Great Commission of our Lord Jesus Christ as stated in Matthew 28:18–20, and elsewhere. To this end, every member shall be urged to take the gospel of salvation to the lost, personally and representatively. Converts shall be instructed as to their duty to confess Christ by baptism (immersion in water), and taught in matters of Christian conduct, Bible study, church attendance, personal soulwinning, tithes and offerings, faithfulness to Christ, and any other areas of instruction deemed necessary to their spiritual prosperity and growth. This shall be further facilitated through the holding of regular and special church services.

(C) The church shall also ordain and license men to the Gospel ministry; educate believers in a manner consistent with the requirements of the Holy Scriptures, both in Sunday and weekday and weeknight schools of Christian education; maintain missionary activities in the United States and in any foreign country; and engage in any other ministry that the church may decide, from time to time, to pursue in obedience to the will of God. (1 Corinthians 7:17, 14:19; Titus 1:5, 2:4; Acts 5:42, 13:1–3, 14:23, 15:35–36, 40, 20:20; 1 Timothy 1:3, 2:7, 3:2, 4:11, 6:2; 2 Timothy 2:2,24; Romans 10:14–15; 2 Corinthians 8:12, 14; Philippians 4:10, 14–16; Hebrews 13:7, 17; Jeremiah 3:15; Ephesians 4:11–12)

ARTICLE 2—STATEMENT OF FAITH AND COVENANT

SECTION 2.01—STATEMENT OF FAITH

The following comprise the Scriptural beliefs of this church and its members.

(A)   The Bible
We believe the Bible to be the revealed Word of God, fully and verbally inspired of God. We believe the Scriptures to be the inerrant, infallible Word of God, as found within the sixty-six books from Genesis to Revelation. We believe that God not only inspired every word, but that He has preserved them through the ages. We believe that the King James Version is the preserved Word of God for the English-speaking people and is the only acceptable translation to be used in this church. (Psalm 12:6–7; 2 Timothy 3:15–17; 1 Peter 1:23–25; 2 Peter 1:19–21)

(B)   God
We believe in one God; Who is eternal, self-existent, infinite, and immutable. We believe He has one nature, one essence, and one substance; yet manifests Himself to man in three Persons: the Father, the Son, and the Holy Spirit. (Deuteronomy 6:4; 1 Timothy 1:17; James 1:17; 1 John 4:4)

(C)   Jesus Christ

We believe Jesus Christ to be the one and only Saviour of mankind. We believe Jesus Christ to be eternally God and to possess all the attributes of Deity. We believe that the Lord Jesus Christ was virgin-born, that He was God incarnate, and that the purposes of the incarnation were to reveal God, to redeem men, and to rule over God's kingdom. We believe Jesus Christ never relinquished any attributes of His Deity, but merely veiled them. We believe He lived a perfect, sinless life, at the end of which He was offered for all mankind as a substitutionary sacrifice for man's sin. This sacrifice was a just payment to God for the forgiveness of sin. It was activated by His death through the shedding of His blood on the cross and was accepted by God upon His resurrection. We believe He ascended into Heaven after His resurrection to be seated at the right hand of the Father and is now waiting for the time of receiving His church at the rapture, which is followed by His return seven years later to earth to rule and reign as King for 1,000 years. (Psalm 2:7–9; Isaiah 7:14, 9:6, 43:11; Micah 5:2; Matthew 1:25; Luke 1:26–35; John 1:1, 1:3, 14, 18, 29; Romans 3:19–25, 5:6–15; Philippians 2:5–11; 1 Thessalonians 4:13–18; 1 Timothy 2:5, 3:16; Titus 2:10–15; Hebrews 7:26, 9:24–28; 1 Peter 1:19, 2:2; 1 John 1:3; Revelation 20:1–6)

(D)   The Holy Spirit

We believe the Holy Spirit of God is a person who has personality and all the attributes of Deity. We believe the Holy Spirit has always been involved in the affairs of mankind; however, we believe He has a special ministry that began at Pentecost and will continue until the rapture. This ministry includes reproving the world of sin, righteousness, and judgment. The Holy Spirit was also sent to regenerate, sanctify, seal, and fill all who have placed their faith in Jesus Christ. (Genesis 1:2; John 3:5–6, 14:16; Acts 1:5, 11:15; 1 Corinthians 3:16, 6:19–20, 12:13)

(E)   Sin and Salvation

We believe all men were born with an inherited sin nature received from our common ancestor, Adam. We believe that because of his nature, man is a sinner by choice, and he is totally incapable of reforming himself or ceasing from his sin by his own power. We believe the only hope of deliverance for man is a total change of mind concerning his sinful condition and inability to change it, and a turning to Jesus Christ as the only Saviour. We believe that only through the substitutionary sacrifice of Christ on the cross can a man be delivered from his sin. We believe that all those who reject Jesus Christ as their Saviour are already condemned to an eternity in the lake of fire. (Genesis 5:1–5; Acts 4:19, 16:31; Romans 3:10–23, 5:6–12, 6:23, 10:9–10; Ephesians 2:8–9; Titus 3:5–6; Revelation 20:11–14)

(F)   The New Testament Church

We believe that the church began with the calling out of the twelve apostles by Jesus Christ and was empowered on the day of Pentecost. We believe the local church is composed of members who have been saved and baptized according to the command of Christ, and have voluntarily united together for the purposes of worship, fellowship, service, and observance of the ordinances of baptism and communion. We believe all true believers will be taken up at the rapture, just prior to the tribulation. (Matthew 16:16–18; Acts 1:15, 2:41–43, 11:15, 20:28; 1 Corinthians 15:51 58; Ephesians 1:12–14, 5:25–30; 1 Thessalonians 4:13–18; 1 Timothy 3:4–15)

(G)   The Last Days

We believe in the literal interpretation of the Scriptures in their grammatical and historical context. We believe in the pre-tribulational rapture of the church saints, followed by the seven-year tribulation. We believe in the pre-millennial return of Christ to the earth and His literal rule of one thousand years. Following this one-thousand-year reign is the Great White Throne judgment and then the new heaven and new earth. (1 Corinthians 15:51–58; 1 Thessalonians 4:13–18, 5:1–9; Revelation 19–22)

(H) Separation

We believe that all the saved should live in such a manner as not to bring reproach upon their Saviour and Lord. God commands His people to separate from all religious apostasy, all worldly and sinful pleasures, practices, and associations; and to refrain from all immodest and immoderate appearances, piercings, and bodily markings. (Romans 12:1–2, 14:13; 2 Corinthians 6:14–7:1; 2 Timothy 3:1–5; 1 John 2:15–17; 2 John 9–11; Leviticus 19:28; 1 Corinthians 6:19–20)

(I) Creation

We believe that God created the universe in six literal, 24-hour periods. We reject evolution, the gap theory, the day-age theory, theistic evolution, and intelligent design not attributed to God as unscriptural theories of origin. (Genesis 1–2; Exodus 20:11)

(J) Civil Government

We believe that God has ordained and created all authority consisting of three basic institutions: 1) the home, 2) the church, and 3) the state. Every person is subject to these authorities, but all (including the authorities themselves) are answerable to God and governed by His Word. God has given each institution specific Biblical responsibilities and balanced these responsibilities with the understanding that no institution has the right to infringe upon the other. The home, the church, and the state are equal and sovereign in their respective biblically-assigned spheres of responsibility under God. (Romans 13:1–7; Ephesians 5:22–24; Hebrews 13:17; 1 Peter 2:13–14)

(K)   Human Sexuality

1.   We believe that God has commanded that no intimate sexual activity be engaged in outside of a marriage between a man and a woman. We believe that any form of homosexuality, lesbianism, bisexuality, bestiality, incest, fornication, adultery, and pornography are sinful perversions of God's gift of sex. We believe that God disapproves of and forbids any attempt to alter one's gender by surgery or appearance. (Genesis 2:24, 19:5, 13, 26:8–9; Leviticus 18:1–30; Romans 1:26–29; 1 Corinthians 5:1; 6:9; 1 Thessalonians 4:1–8; Hebrews 13:4)

2.   We believe that the only legitimate marriage is the joining of one man and one woman. (Genesis 2:24; Romans 7:2; 1 Corinthians 7:10; Ephesians 5:22–23)

3.   In keeping with our beliefs regarding human sexuality as expressed in this statement of faith and in keeping with our purpose as expressed in Section 1.02, we have the following practical policies:

a.   All people are welcome to attend our regular worship services.

b.   Those who attend may not display behavior that is indicative of the sinful behaviors listed in (K)(1) of this section in church services, at church functions, and on the church grounds.

c.   Church representatives are not to display overt disrespect for those who are involved in the sinful behaviors listed in (K)(1) of this section.

d.   The pastor of the church will preach consistently against all forms of sinful behavior as listed in (K)(1) of this section, as well as other sinful behaviors.

(L)   Family Relationships

1.   We believe that men and women are spiritually equal in position before God but that God has ordained distinct and separate spiritual functions for men and women in the home and in the church. The husband is to be the leader of the home, and men are to be the leaders (pastors and deacons) of the church. Accordingly, only men are eligible for licensure and ordination by the church. (Galatians 3:28; Colossians 3:18; 1 Timothy 2:8–15, 3:4–5, 12)

2.   We believe that God has ordained the family as the foundational institution of human society. The husband is to love his wife as Christ loves the church. The wife is to submit herself to the Scriptural leadership of her husband as the church submits to the headship of Christ. Children are an heritage from the Lord. Parents are responsible for teaching their children spiritual and moral values and leading them, through consistent lifestyle example and appropriate discipline, including Scriptural corporal correction. (Genesis 1:26–28; Exodus 20:12; Deuteronomy 6:4–9; Psalm 127:3–5; Proverbs 19:18, 22:15, 23:13–14; Mark 10:6–12; 1 Corinthians 7:1–16; Ephesians 5:21–33, 6:1–4, Colossians 3:18–21; Hebrews 13:4; 1 Peter 3:1–7)

(M)   Divorce and Remarriage

We believe that God disapproves of and forbids divorce and intends marriage to last until one of the spouses dies. Although divorced and remarried persons or divorced persons may hold positions of service in the church and be greatly used of God for Christian service, they may not be considered for the offices of pastor or deacon or those administrative positions within the church that would consist of pastoral duties. (Malachi 2:14–17; Matthew 19:3–12; Romans 7:1–3; 1 Timothy 3:2, 12; Titus 1:6)

(N) **Abortion**

We believe that human life begins at conception and that the unborn child is a living human being. Abortion constitutes the unjustified, unexcused taking of unborn human life. Abortion is murder. We reject any teaching that abortions of pregnancies due to rape, incest, birth defects, gender selection, birth or population control, or the physical or mental well being of the mother are acceptable. (Job 3:16; Psalm 51:5; 139:14–16; Isaiah 44:24, 49:1, 5; Jeremiah 1:5, 20:15–18; Luke 1:44)

(O) **Love**

We believe that we should demonstrate love for others, not only toward fellow believers, but also toward both those who are not believers and those who oppose us. We are to deal with those who oppose us graciously, gently, patiently, and humbly. God forbids the stirring up of strife, the taking of revenge, or the threat or the use of violence as a means of resolving personal conflict or obtaining personal justice. Although God commands us to abhor sinful actions, we are to love and pray for any person who engages in such sinful actions. (Leviticus 19:18; Matthew 5:44–48; Luke 6:31; John 13:34–35; Romans 12:9–10, 17–21, 13:8–10; Philippians 2:2–4; 2 Timothy 2:24–26; Titus 3:2; 1 John 3:17–18)

(P) **Lawsuits between Believers**

We believe that Christians are prohibited from bringing civil lawsuits against other Christians or the church to resolve personal disputes. We believe the church possesses all the resources necessary to resolve personal disputes between members. We do believe, however, that a Christian may seek compensation for injuries from another Christian's insurance company as long as the claim is pursued without malice or slander. (1 Corinthians 6:1–8; Ephesians 4:31–32)

(Q)   Missions
We believe that God has given the church a great commission to proclaim the Gospel to all nations so that there might be a great multitude from every nation, tribe, ethnic group, and language group who believe on the Lord Jesus Christ. As ambassadors of Christ we must use all available means to go to the foreign nations and not wait for them to come to us. (Matthew 28:19–20; Mark 16:15; Luke 24:46–48; John 20:21; Acts 1:8; 2 Corinthians 5:20)

(R)   Giving
We believe that every Christian, as a steward of that portion of God's wealth entrusted to him, is obligated to support his local church financially. We believe that God has established the tithe as a basis for giving, but that every Christian should also give other offerings sacrificially and cheerfully to the support of the church, the relief of those in need, and the spread of the Gospel. We believe that a Christian relinquishes all rights to direct the use of the tithe or offering once the gift has been made. (Genesis 14:20; Proverbs 3:9–10; Acts 4:34–37; 1 Corinthians 16:2; 2 Corinthians 9:6–7; Galatians 6:6; Ephesians 4:28; 1 Timothy 5:17–18; 1 John 3:17)

(S)   Euthanasia
We believe that the direct taking of an innocent human life is a moral evil, regardless of the intention. Life is a gift of God and must be respected from conception until natural death. Thus we believe that an act or omission which, of itself or by intention, causes death in order to eliminate suffering constitutes a murder contrary to the will of God. Discontinuing medical procedures that are extraordinary or disproportionate to the expected outcome can be a

legitimate refusal of over-zealous treatment. (Exodus 20:13, 23:7; Matthew 5:21; Acts 17:28)

SECTION 2.02—AUTHORITY OF STATEMENT OF FAITH

The Bible (King James Version) itself is the final authority in all matters of faith and practice of what we believe. The Statement of Faith does not exhaust the extent of our faith. We do believe, however, that the foregoing Statement of Faith accurately represents the teaching of the Bible and, therefore, is binding upon all members.

SECTION 2.03—COVENANT

Having been led, as we believe, by the Spirit of God, to receive the Lord Jesus Christ as our Saviour, and on profession of our faith, having been baptized in the name of our Father, and of the Son, and of the Holy Ghost, we do now, in the presence of God, angels, and this assembly, most solemnly and joyfully enter into covenant with one another, as one body in Christ.

We engage, therefore, by the aid of the Holy Spirit, to walk together in Christian love; to strive for the advancement of this church in knowledge, holiness and comfort; to promote its prosperity and spirituality; to sustain its worship, ordinances, discipline and doctrines; to give it a sacred preeminence over all institutions of human origin; and to contribute cheerfully and regularly to the support of the ministry, the expenses of the church, the relief of the poor, and the spread of the Gospel through all nations.

We also engage to maintain family and private devotions; to religiously educate our children; to seek the salvation of our kindred, acquaintances, and all others; to walk circumspectly in the world; to be just in our dealings, faithful to our engagements, and exemplary in our deportment; to avoid all tattling, backbiting, and excessive anger; to abstain from worldly amusements; to be free from all oath-bound secret societies and partnerships with unbelievers; to abstain from the sale or use of narcotic drugs; and to be zealous in our efforts to advance the Kingdom of our Saviour. Other standards or leadership requirements, as approved by the pastor and deacons, for Christian living, will be addressed for those serving in positions of ministry leadership.

We further engage to watch over one another in brotherly love; to remember each other in prayer; to aid each other in sickness and distress; to cultivate Christian sympathy in feeling and courtesy of speech; to be slow to take offense, but always ready for reconciliation, and mindful of the rules of our Saviour, and to secure reconciliation without delay.

We moreover engage, that when we remove from this place, we will as soon as possible unite with some other Baptist church where we can carry out the spirit of this covenant and the principles of God's Word.

ARTICLE 3—MEMBERSHIP

SECTION 3.01—QUALIFICATIONS FOR MEMBERSHIP

Upon a majority vote of the members present at any church service or meeting, membership shall be extended to all who have had and whose lives evidence a genuine experience of regeneration through faith in and acceptance of the Lord Jesus Christ as personal Saviour; who renounce sin; who endeavor to live a consecrated life wholly unto the Lord; who fully subscribe to the Statement of Faith contained herein; who enter into the church covenant contained herein; who agree to submit to the authority of the church and its leaders as set forth herein; and upon compliance with any one of the following conditions and with compliance to the additional requirements stated in the final paragraph of this section:

(A)   By baptism (immersion) as a true believer in Christ Jesus as personal Saviour;

(Any person that places his faith in Jesus as the Son of God—Who died and shed His blood on the cross to atone for our sins—and that accepts Him as his own Saviour, and with all his heart is willing to obey Him and His Word, may, by acknowledgement of the church and by baptism, be received into membership, per Acts 2:41);

(B)   By letter of transfer from another Bible-believing Baptist church of like faith and practice if the applicant has been baptized by immersion subsequent to a profession of faith;

(C)   By testimony of faith, having been baptized by immersion under the authority of another Bible-believing Baptist church of like faith and practice (Acts 9:18, 26–27; 1 Timothy 1:16); or

(D)   By restoration, if having been removed from membership, upon majority vote of the congregation after confession is made publicly before the church membership of the sin or sins involved, and satisfactorily evidencing repentance to the pastor (or the board of deacons if the office of pastor is vacant) (Galatians 6:1–2; James 5:16).

It is our policy that those unrepentantly committed to a lifestyle in violation of the tenets of faith and covenant of Article 2 or other Scriptural prohibitions will not be considered for membership. In all cases those living a lifestyle exhibiting the perversions described in Section 2.01(K)(1) will not be considered for membership. In all cases, the pastor (or board of deacons, if the office of pastor is vacant) reserves the right to refuse membership consideration to any person or persons whose lifestyle is not consistent with a personal relationship with the Lord. The authority to make such a decision may be delegated to a pastoral staff member of the church in conjunction with some or all of the deacons at the discretion of the pastor.

SECTION 3.02—DUTIES OF A MEMBER

On becoming a member of this church, in addition to the covenant contained in Article 2, Section 2.03, each one further covenants to love, honor, and esteem the pastor; to pray for him; to recognize his authority in spiritual affairs of the church; to cherish a brotherly love (John 13:35) for all members of the church; to support the church in prayer, tithes, offerings and with other financial support as the Lord enables; and in accordance with Biblical commands, to support through a lifestyle walk affirming the beliefs and practices of the church.

(A) It is the duty of members to love, to honor, and to esteem the pastor (1 Thessalonians 5:12–13), to pray for him (2 Thessalonians 3:1–2), and to submit to him in the Scriptural exercise of his Holy Spirit-given authority (Acts 20:28; Hebrews 13:7, 17).

(B) Toward those outside the membership, it is the duty of members to be exact in fulfilling obligations, keeping promises, and, as opportunity enables, to commend the Gospel of Christ to such persons.

(C) It is the duty of members, upon moving from this area, to unite with another Baptist church of like faith and practice and to request that church to send to Lancaster Baptist Church for their letters of recommendation.

SECTION 3.03—PRIVILEGES OF MEMBERSHIP

(A) Only members at least 18 (eighteen) years of age who are physically present at a duly called meeting of the church shall be entitled to vote. There shall be no proxy or absentee voting. The eligible membership of the church has certain limited areas to exercise a vote. Members may not vote to initiate any church action, rather the vote of a member is to confirm and ratify the direction of the church as determined by the pastor. (Acts 13:1–2)

(B)   This congregation functions not as a pure democracy, but as a body under the Headship of the Lord Jesus Christ and the direction of the pastor as the undershepherd with the counsel of the board of deacons. Determinations of the internal affairs of this church are ecclesiastical matters and shall be determined exclusively by the church's own rules and procedures. The pastor shall oversee and/or conduct all aspects of this church. The board of deacons shall give counsel and assistance to the pastor as requested by him.

(C)   Membership in this church does not afford the members with any property, contractual, or civil rights based on principles of democratic government. Although the general public is invited to all of the church's worship services, the church property remains private property. The pastor (or in his absence, an individual designated by the board of deacons) has the authority to suspend or revoke the right of any person, including a member, to enter or remain on church property. If after being notified of such a suspension or revocation the person enters or remains on church property, the person may, in the discretion of the pastor (or in his absence, an individual designated by the board of deacons), be treated as a trespasser.

(D)   A member may request an appointment with the financial administrator to ask questions or to discuss church finances. Financial records shall be distributed for inspection in accordance with the duties of the financial administrator as specified in Section 5.03.

(E)   Individual giving records, individual membership records, counseling records, staff compensation records, employee files, the minutes of the meetings of the board of deacons, and other personal and/or confidential records shall not be available for inspection or copying.

SECTION 3.04—DISCIPLINE OF A MEMBER

(A)   There shall be a discipline committee consisting of the pastor or a member of the pastoral staff and either all or part of the board of deacons. These men shall have sole authority in determining heretical deviations from the Statement of Faith, violations of the church covenant, or any habitual behavior that is unbecoming to a saint of God. The pastor and deacons may bring an individual who is unrepentant and unwilling to be restored before the church body for dismissal. If the pastor or a deacon is the subject of a disciplinary matter, he shall not sit as a member of the discipline committee. The pastor and deacons shall be entitled to the same steps as other church members and be subject to the same discipline.

(B)   Members are expected to demonstrate special loyalty and concern for one another. When a member becomes aware of an offense of such magnitude that it hinders spiritual growth and testimony, he is to go alone to the offending party and seek to restore his brother. Before he goes, he should first examine himself. When he goes, he should go with a spirit of humility and have the goal of restoration.

(C)   If reconciliation is not reached, a second member, either a deacon or a member of the pastoral staff (or a wife of a pastoral staff member at the pastor's discretion for matters solely between ladies) is to accompany the one seeking to resolve the matter. This second step should also be preceded by self-examination and exercised in a spirit of humility with the goal of restoration.

(D)   If the matter is still unresolved after the steps outlined in subsections (B) and (C) have been taken, the discipline committee, as the church representatives who are biblically responsible for putting down murmuring, shall hear the matter. If the matter is not resolved during the hearing before the discipline committee, the committee shall recommend to the members of the church that they, after self-examination, make an effort personally to go to the offending member and seek that member's restoration.

(E)   If the matter is still unresolved after the steps outlined in subsections (B), (C), and (D) have been taken, such members who refuse to repent and be restored are to be removed from the membership of the church upon a majority vote of the membership present at a meeting called for the purpose of considering disciplinary action.

(F)   No matter may be heard by the discipline committee or the church unless the steps outlined in subsections (B) and (C) have been taken, except in the case of a public offense.

(G)   If an unrepentant offending party is removed from the church membership, all contact with him from that point forward (except by family members) must be for the sake of restoration.

(H)   The procedures provided in this section are based on Matthew 18:15–20; Romans 16:17–18; 1 Corinthians 5:1–13; 2 Corinthians 2:1–11; Galatians 6:1; 1 Thessalonians 5:14; 2 Thessalonians 3:6, 10–15; 1 Timothy 5:19–20; and Titus 3:10–11.

(I)   Member participation in any meeting which pertains to church administration—other than those meetings authorized by Article 6 or those conducted by church officers and employees in the course of their official duties—shall be cause for automatic discipline of those members involved. (1 Corinthians 5:1–5, 9–13; 2 John 9–11)

(J)   Membership may be terminated pursuant to this section as a result of immorality, drunkenness, discord, gossip, heresies, or any habitual behavior that is unbecoming to a saint of

God. (Psalm 15:1,3; Matthew 18:15–17; 1 Corinthians 5:11, 13; 2 Thessalonians 3:11–12; 1 Timothy 5:13, 15, 6:3–5; 1 Peter 4:15)

SECTION 3.05—TRANSFER OF MEMBERSHIP

Members not under the disciplinary process of Section 3.04 may request that letters of transfer be sent to another church.

SECTION 3.06—TERMINATION OF MEMBERSHIP

(A)   Delinquency: Any member who avoidably misses services for a period of six months, typically based on the record of class attendance, shall be known as delinquent, and the said member's name shall be presented to the pastoral staff and/or deacons, as such. The pastoral staff and/or deacons, having made investigation, and the said condition not corrected nor cause found for the delinquency, shall then, without unnecessary delay (typically within 1–2 weeks), place such a member on inactive status. Members on inactive status have no voting privileges or say in church meetings at all. Members not on inactive status are active members. The pastoral staff and/or deacons, having witnessed a period of renewed faithfulness in attendance of the inactive member, may, at their discretion, return the person's status to being an active member.

(B)   Dual Membership: No member of this church may hold membership in another church simultaneously. If any member unites in membership with another church, that person is automatically terminated without notice from membership in this church.

(C)   Resignation: A member may resign at any time, but no letter of transfer or written statement of good standing will be issued upon such resignation, except at the discretion of the pastor.

(D)   Automatic: Automatic termination of church membership shall occur for any church member committing an act of homosexuality, lesbianism, bisexuality, bestiality, incest, adultery, or change of gender through surgery or appearance or shall occur for any church member who promotes such activities as these or who promotes activities involving fornication or pornography or shall occur for any church member who expresses publicly that any one of these such behaviors is his or her continued way of life.

(E)   Discipline: Membership may be terminated as a result of discipline of the member in accordance with Section 3.04.

(F)   Death: Upon the death of a church member, the member's status on the church roll shall state that the said member is deceased.

(G)   Letter of Transfer: Membership in this church shall be terminated upon a letter of transfer being sent to another church, in accordance with Section 3.05.

ARTICLE 4—OFFICERS

SECTION 4.01—CHURCH OFFICERS

Based on the New Testament model of the local church, the church has two Biblical officers: pastor (Section 5.01) and deacon (Section 5.02). No person may hold both of these offices simultaneously.

Various administrative responsibilities are delegated to employees, as an extension of the pastor's office. These positions include, but are not limited to, the financial administrator (Section 5.03) and associate pastors (Section 5.04). All members of the church staff are considered to be an extension of the pastor's ministry and under his supervision (Sections 4.06[B] and 5.01[E]).

SECTION 4.02—DESIGNATION OF CORPORATE OFFICERS

As an accommodation to legal relationships outside the church, the pastor shall serve as the president of the corporation; the financial administrator shall serve as treasurer of the corporation; a deacon appointed by the pastor and deacons shall serve as vice-president of the corporation; and a deacon appointed by the pastor and deacons shall serve as the secretary of the corporation. Only these individuals may legally bind the corporation.

SECTION 4.03—ELIGIBILITY FOR OFFICE

(A)   The church shall not install or retain an officer who fails to adhere to or expresses disagreement with the Statement of Faith. All church officers, upon request of the pastor, shall affirm their agreement with the Statement of Faith (as set forth in Article 2).

(B)   All church officers must be approved initially by the pastor in order for them to commence in their offices.

(C)   Only active church members are eligible for election or appointment to any church office or position.

SECTION 4.04—TERMS OF OFFICE

(A)   The term of the pastor shall be for an undesignated period of time; he shall not be subject to dismissal by the church at any time, except for violation(s) of the Statement of Faith or church bylaws. The calling of a pastor may be considered at any regular church administration meeting, provided notice to that effect shall have been given from the pulpit to the church two Sundays prior to said regular church administration meeting. A three-fourths majority of the active members present and voting shall be required to call a pastor. Disciplinary removal of the pastor from office automatically terminates his membership. A restoration to membership after disciplinary removal will be subject to the requirements of Section 3.01(D).

(B) The term of service for deacons in the church shall be two years, at the expiration of which they may be re-elected. The financial administrator shall be a paid employee of the church who is hired with the approval of the pastor.

(C) A vacancy occurring in any office or board, except in the case of the pastor, may be filled at any regular church administration meeting or worship service, at the discretion of the pastor.

(D) All elected and appointed officers shall serve in their respective offices until their successors are duly elected or appointed.

(E) Members of the board of deacons may be removed from office for unbiblical conduct, as determined by the other board members, upon a majority vote of the remaining members of the board of deacons.

SECTION 4.05—ELECTION OF DEACONS

The annual election of deacons by the church membership shall occur during the month of January at the annual church administration meeting (Victory Meeting). Two groups exist within the board of deacons, with each group voted upon in alternating years due to the two-year terms being served. All deacons eligible for re-election, as well as those new nominees each year, are voted upon with either a "for" or an "against" vote; thus, this is a non-competitive election.

SECTION 4.06—PASTORAL OVERSIGHT OF OFFICERS AND STAFF

(A)   The pastor may hire associates and assistants to assist the pastor in carrying out his God-given responsibilities, as well as any related support staff. The pastor will communicate with the deacons regarding positions which need to be filled.

(B)   All church staff, whether paid or volunteer, shall be under the supervision of the pastor who has the sole authority to dismiss the same. No employee or volunteer shall be hired, appointed, or retained who fails to adhere to or expresses disagreement with the Statement of Faith or who is not a member of Lancaster Baptist Church.

ARTICLE 5—DUTIES AND POWERS OF OFFICERS

SECTION 5.01—THE PASTOR

(A)   The pastor shall preach the Gospel regularly and shall be at liberty to preach the whole counsel of the Word of God as the Lord leads him. He shall administer the ordinances of the church, act as moderator at all church meetings for the transaction of church matters, supervise the teaching ministries of the church, and tenderly watch over the spiritual interests of the membership.

(B)   The pastor shall appoint the members of the various committees as needed throughout the year. He shall serve as the president of the corporation. He shall inform all newly elected and/or hired officers of the particular function and the responsibilities of their respective offices. He shall extend the right hand of fellowship to all new members on behalf of the church and perform such other duties as generally appertain to such a position. The pastor shall be free to choose the means and methods by which he exercises the ministry that God has given him.

(C) All appointments for public worship and Bible study and the arrangements thereof, including time and place and the use of the property belonging to the church for purposes other than the stated appointments, shall be under the control of the pastor.

(D) The pastor is an undershepherd or Spiritual overseer. The Scriptures also refer to this office as elder or bishop (Acts 20:28; 1 Thessalonians 5:12–13; 1 Timothy 3:1–5, 5:17; Hebrews 13:7–17; 1 Peter 5:1–4). These are examples of such and also show clearly that the pastor is to oversee and supervise the affairs of the church. He shall not only have the general supervision of the church, but shall have unrestricted liberty in presenting any matter he deems necessary to the church for its consideration and instruction.

(E) It shall be the responsibility of the pastor to perform the various duties incumbent on his office. He shall be solely responsible for the hiring, firing, disciplining, and supervising of all employees connected in any way with the church. This includes voluntary, voted, and hired help. He shall be free to act without imposition of defending his actions in this regard (Hebrews 13:17).

(F) He shall be the moderator of the church and preside at all of its administration meetings. He shall be an ex-officio member of all the committees, organizations, and societies within the church, including the privilege of voting. He shall be in charge of the pulpit and be held responsible for supplying speakers. In legal matters he shall act as president of the corporation (Acts 15:3–7, 12).

(G) First Timothy 3:1–6 and Titus 1:7–9 give the qualifications of a pastor. The life of the pastor and his family shall be an example of godliness and Spirituality. They shall not indulge in worldly or sinful practices, as these would weaken the testimony of the church (1 Thessalonians 5:22). No one who uses intoxicating liquors, drugs, or tobacco in any form, or who brings disrepute upon his ministry through sinful language, practice, or associations shall be considered for pastor.

(H) Because of this office, the pastor shall be counted worthy of double honor (1 Timothy 5:17). No accusations shall be accepted against him without at least two or three witnesses (1 Timothy 5:19).

(I) No divorced person shall be pastor of the church. No person shall be considered for the office nor serve as pastor of this church whose beliefs and teachings are not in accordance with the Statement of Faith, or who will not declare himself to be a Fundamental, Pre-Millenial, Independent Baptist (1 Timothy 3:1–2; Titus 1:5–6).

(J) No person shall be considered for nor serve as pastor who maintains any connection with the National Council of Churches (NCC); the World Council of Churches (WCC); or any agency, convention, or other ecclesiastical body of either the NCC or WCC.

(K) No woman shall be considered for nor serve as pastor of this church (1 Timothy 2:12, 3:2).

(L) The pastor shall certify and keep at the office of the church, the original bylaws or a copy, including all amendments or alterations to the bylaws;

(M) Shall keep at the place where the bylaws or a copy are kept, a record of the proceedings of meetings of the board of deacons, with the times and places of holding, the notices of meetings given, and the names of those present at the meetings;

(N) Exhibit at all reasonable times to proper persons on terms provided by law the bylaws and minutes of proceedings of the board of deacons or the minutes of the meetings of the church members;

(O) Shall see that all notices are duly given in accordance with the provisions of these bylaws;

(P) Shall keep an account of any special events in the life of the church which are of historical interest;

(Q) Be custodian of the records of the church, including the membership roll, baptisms, and certificates of ordination, licenses and commissions.

SECTION 5.02—THE DEACONS

(A) The word, which in the King James Version is translated *deacons*, according to the Strong's Exhaustive Concordance of the Bible, means "servant, attendant, aid, waiter, etc." The meaning given for the word *deacon* in 1 Timothy 3:10 and 13 is "to be an attendant, to wait upon." The Greek words translated *deacons* in Philippians 1:1 and 1 Timothy 3:8–12 are given to mean "to run errands, an attendant, a waiter, specifically to a Christian teacher and pastor." In Acts 6:1–4, the first servants were chosen by the church for the purpose of performing such tasks as would free those in charge of the services for prayer and the study of the Word. Therefore, because this church accepts the Scriptures as final authority rather than tradition, the office of deacon shall not in any way be taken to mean authority over the church and pastor.

(B) The general duties of a deacon, aside from appointed tasks, shall be to assist the pastor in building up the church numerically, financially, and Spiritually; to visit the sick, sorrowing, and needy; to prepare for the observance of the Lord's Table; to strive personally to win the lost to Christ; to guard and protect the reputation of the church and pastor against gossip; to investigate delinquents, and to endeavor to remedy any Spiritual weakness in the lives of the members; to cooperate with the pastor in the care, operation, and repair of the physical properties of the church; and to care for the administrative needs of the church's various ministries as requested by the pastor.

(C)   Duties toward the pastor shall be to pray for him earnestly and continually; to see that his material and physical needs are taken care of; and to strive in every way to help him in the performance of Scriptural duties (Acts 6:2–7).

(D)   First Timothy 3:8–13 gives the qualifications of a deacon and his wife. In their lifestyles, a deacon and his family shall not indulge in worldly and sinful practices that would tend to weaken the testimony of this church (1 Thessalonians 5:22). No one who uses intoxicating liquors, drugs, or tobacco; or who brings disrepute upon the church through sinful language, practice, or associations, shall be considered for deacon or, having fallen into such practices and persisting in the same, be retained. Habitual disobedience of the Word of God shall disqualify the deacon, and his office shall be declared vacant upon such a determination by the pastor and/or balance of the board of deacons. Also, in keeping with the Scriptures, gossiping, tattling, back-biting, undermining, holding grudges, violent uncontrolled temper, etc. are unbecoming of the office of a deacon and, if indulged in by either a deacon or his wife, shall be grounds for dismissal from office at the discretion of the pastor and/or board of deacons.

(E)   No person shall be elected to the office of deacon who has not been a faithful member of the church for a period of one year or more (1 Timothy 3:10).

(F) A deacon is to be faithful in all things (1 Timothy 3:11), especially the regular and special services of the church. Therefore, unless because of illness or otherwise providentially hindered, a deacon is expected to attend all church, victory, and deacons meetings. Habitual absence from these meetings at the discretion of the pastor and board of deacons shall disqualify the deacon, and his office shall be declared vacant.

(G) Each deacon shall be elected for a term of two years. He may be re-elected as many times as the pastor and the church so desire.

(H) New deacons shall be nominated by the currently serving deacons, who will serve as the nominating committee.

(I) The board of deacons shall constitute the board of trustees of the corporation. The board of trustees shall exercise only the following specific powers, upon expressed approval by the pastor and upon authorization by a majority vote of the members present at a duly called church administration meeting:

1. To purchase, hold, lease, or otherwise acquire real and personal property on behalf of the church, and to take real and personal property by will, gift, or bequest on behalf of the church;

2. To sell, convey, alienate, transfer, lease, assign, exchange, or otherwise dispose of, and to mortgage, pledge, or otherwise encumber the real and personal property of the church; to borrow money and incur indebtedness for the purpose and the use of the church; to cause to be executed, issued, and delivered for the indebtedness, in the name of the church, promissory notes, bonds, debentures, or other evidence of indebtedness; and to secure

repayment by deeds of trust, mortgages, or pledges; and

3. To exercise all powers necessary for the dissolution of the church corporation.

(J) The currently serving deacons of the church shall meet with the pastor prior to the election at the annual victory meeting and, after prayer, shall select men from among the non-paid, church employee membership who meet the requirements and who will cooperate with the leadership in fulfilling the duties of the office. The nominees shall meet with the pastor before their names are placed on the ballot or read before the church prior to voting. These men must be nominated ahead of time and their names placed on the ballot in order to be elected at the annual election. Vacancies may be filled at any regular or special administration meeting of the church, at the discretion of the pastor.

SECTION 5.03—THE FINANCIAL ADMINISTRATOR

The financial administrator shall be interviewed and hired by the pastor in cooperation with the deacons of the church. The financial administrator shall:

(A) Have charge and custody of, and be responsible for, all funds of the corporation, and deposit all funds in the name of the church in banks, trust companies, or other depositories as shall be selected by the pastor or the board of deacons;

(B) Receive, and give receipt for all contributions, gifts, and donations to the church;

(C) Disburse, or cause to be disbursed, the funds of the church as may be directed by the pastor, the board of deacons, or the budget adopted by the members of the church at the annual church administration meeting (Victory Meeting), taking proper vouchers for the disbursements;

(D)   Keep and maintain adequate and correct accounts of the church's properties and business transactions including account of its assets, liabilities, receipts, disbursements, and capital;

(E)   When and as requested, render to the pastor and the board of deacons an account of all transactions and of the financial condition of the church;

(F)   Present a written report of receipts, disbursements, assets, and liabilities for all ministries (e.g., church, college, school, publications, etc.) at the regular monthly meeting of the board of deacons;

(G)   Present a written, summarized report of receipts and disbursements for the church ministry only at the annual church administration meeting (Victory Meeting);

(H)   Keep all financial records at the office of the church or in a secure, pastor and board of deacons approved, offsite storage facility, and deliver them to any successor upon leaving office;

(I)   Serve as treasurer of the corporation;

(K)   Sign, certify, or attest documents as may be required by law;

(L)   See that the reports, statements, certificates, and all other documents and records required by law are properly kept and filed.

SECTION 5.04—ASSOCIATE PASTORS

Under the direction and guidance of the pastor, the associate pastor(s) of the church shall assist the pastor in carrying out the ministries of the church.

SECTION 5.05—DUTIES OF ALL OFFICERS

(A) All officers shall prepare a written report of their work for the annual church administration meeting and shall surrender any records in their possession to the pastor at the close of their terms of office to be filed as a permanent record of the work of the church. All records are the property of the church and must be kept in the church office or in a secured off-site storage location accessible by the pastor and financial administrator.

(B) Any officer who neglects his duties as outlined in the bylaws may be removed from his office at the discretion of the pastor, and another may be appointed by the pastor to serve the un-expired term.

SECTION 5.06—CHURCH ATTENDANCE OF PERSONS IN LEADERSHIP

In order to promote a high Spiritual standard for this church, all officers, teachers, and committeemen will be expected to attend all regular services of the church; except they be sick, providentially hindered, on leave, sabbatical, or vacation with pastoral (or board of deacons, if the office of pastor is vacant) approval, or be in attendance at another church of like faith representing the purposes of Lancaster Baptist Church as seen in Section 1.02. An office shall be declared vacant after evident delinquency.

SECTION 5.07—CALL OF THE PASTOR

Whenever necessary, whether by death, resignation, or removal of the pastor, the church shall, without unnecessary delay, proceed to secure a new pastor in the following manner:

(A) The deacons will serve as the pulpit committee. If the church does not have qualified deacons when the office of pastor is vacant, a pulpit committee shall be elected from the membership.

(B) The pulpit committee shall meet and elect one of its members to contact and invite to the pulpit a minister who meets the requirements of the constitution and bylaws. He shall be in accordance with the Statement of Faith. No person shall be invited to the pulpit of the church without consent of the pulpit committee.

(C) It shall be announced in at least one regular public service, previous to the taking of a ballot, that the visiting minister is a candidate for the office of pastor of the church, and the voting time announced.

(D) The vote must be by written and secret ballot.

(E) A three-fourths majority of the active members present and voting shall be necessary for the calling of the pastor.

ARTICLE 6—MEETINGS

SECTION 6.01—MEETINGS FOR WORSHIP

Unless otherwise determined by the pastor, the church shall meet each Sunday for public worship both morning and evening and at least once during the week for Bible study and prayer. The ordinance of the Lord's Supper shall be observed periodically throughout the year, at the discretion of the pastor.

SECTION 6.02—MEETINGS FOR CHURCH ADMINISTRATION

(A) The annual church administration meeting (Victory Meeting) shall be held on the third Wednesday of January each year, unless the pastor determines in advance of this date to have it at another time, at which time the annual victory report of the previous year's blessings shall be presented, the budget for the new year shall be presented and adopted, and the deacons up for election in that year will be voted upon. A quorum shall consist of the active members present.

(B)   All church administration meetings shall be opened and closed with prayer for divine guidance and blessing.

(C)   The moderator shall determine the rules of procedure according to his sense of fairness and common sense, giving all members a reasonable opportunity to be heard on a matter while being careful to protect the privacy of the member asking the question. The moderator is the final authority on questions of procedure, and his decision is final. The following order shall be typical at the annual church administration meeting (Victory Meeting):

1. Wednesday night worship and prayer service concludes
2. Prayer
3. Presentation of the previous year's victory report
4. Presentation of the previous year's receipts and disbursements for the church ministry
5. Presentation of the current year's proposed budget for the church ministry
6. Adoption of the current year's budget for the church ministry
7. Presentation of the previous year's mission support
8. Presentation of nominated deacons
9. Election of deacons
10. Closing prayer

(D)   For any meeting under this article, the moderator, in his sole discretion, shall have full and unilateral authority to require nonmembers to leave the meeting room and to order the immediate removal of any member or other person present who is deemed by the moderator to be disruptive to the proceedings by act or presence. The moderator shall have full authority to order the removal of all children (ages to be determined by the moderator) if the moderator determines, in his sole discretion, that circumstances so warrant. If the moderator determines that compliance with his order of removal is unsatisfactory, the moderator may, in his sole discretion, revoke the disruptive person's right to remain on the premises in accordance with Section 3.03(C) and treat the person as a trespasser.

SECTION 6.03—SPECIAL MEETINGS

(A)   A meeting for the calling of a pastor or the severance of the relationship between the church and pastor shall be called in accordance with the provision of Section 4.04(A).

(B)   Bible conferences, missionary conferences, and revivals may be held as the pastor deems beneficial.

(C)   Special church meetings may be called at any time by the pastor when such meetings fall on regular times of service.

(D)   The pastor may call a special church meeting falling on a time other than the regular church service, providing it is announced in at least one regular service prior to the date of the meeting.

(E)   No secret or unauthorized meetings are permitted. No activity beyond that of routine weekly affairs shall be carried on in the absence of the pastor, unless otherwise directed by the pastor.

(F)   Unless otherwise stipulated in the constitution and bylaws, a majority vote of the voting members at any constitutionally called church meeting shall be required. The minimum voting age is 18 (eighteen).

SECTION 6.04—DEACONS MEETINGS

The meeting of the deacons shall be called by the pastor for the purpose of reviewing the activities of the church. Meetings should be held approximately every four to six weeks, or at the discretion of the pastor.

ARTICLE 7—MINISTRY OF EDUCATION

SECTION 7.01—PURPOSE

The church believes that it is to provide the members and members' children with an education which is based upon and consistent with Biblical teachings. The church believes that the home and church are responsible before God for providing a Christian education. In order to assist the church's families with their obligation to biblically train their children, the church shall operate a Christian day school. To this end, the church shall engage in ministries in education in keeping with the following dictates.

SECTION 7.02—CHURCH PARTICIPATION

All educational programs or courses of instruction formulated and offered by the church shall be primarily for the benefit of the members of the church; however, the pastor may permit non-church members to participate in church educational programs or courses of instruction if he deems it in the best interest of the church. Special classes offered within the church are not open to whoever would choose to attend. The pastor reserves the right to determine who may attend which classes by his own criteria and discretion and may delegate the authority to make such decisions to other pastoral employees of the church, keeping, however, his authority to override any decisions in such matters which may have been made by others.

SECTION 7.03—STAFF MEMBERSHIP

All instructors, teachers, and administrators shall be members of this church. This provision shall not apply to visiting missionaries, evangelists, or preachers engaged for the purpose of delivering sermons, conducting revivals, or other special meetings on a temporary basis.

SECTION 7.04—STATEMENT OF FAITH ACCORD

All educational programs or courses of instruction shall be taught and presented in full accord with the Statement of Faith of the church. The church shall not hire, appoint, or retain any employee or volunteer for its educational programs who fails to adhere to or expresses disagreement with the Statement of Faith.

SECTION 7.05—UNITY

All educational programs or courses of instruction shall be conducted as integral and inseparable ministries of the church.

SECTION 7.06—TEACHING

All educational programs or courses of instruction shall be conducted consistent with the teaching of the inerrant Word of God. Any assertion or belief which conflicts with or questions a Bible truth as interpreted by the pastor is a pagan deception and distortion of the truth which will be disclaimed as false. It is the responsibility of every instructor or teacher to present the inerrant Word of God as the sole infallible source of knowledge and wisdom.

SECTION 7.07—CHRISTIAN WALK

All administrators, instructors, teachers, and other staff, whether paid or volunteer, shall continue or adopt and maintain a lifestyle consistent with the precepts taught by the church, whether in or out of the classroom. All staff shall be under the supervision of the pastor, who has the sole authority to hire, appoint, or dismiss the same as stated herein.

SECTION 7.08—HIERARCHY OF AUTHORITY

(A)   The pastor shall be the final authority on all matters relating to the ministry of education. The pastor shall have the authority to approve or disapprove any decision or recommendation of the board of deacons on all matters relating to the ministry of education.

   1.   On the condition that they shall become members of the church upon assuming duties, the pastor may hire administrators and principals to assist the pastor in carrying out the ministry of education.

   2.   On the condition that they shall become members of the church upon assuming duties, the pastor may hire teachers and support staff to assist the pastor in carrying out the ministry of education.

(B)   The board of deacons shall assist and advise the pastor on all matters relating to the ministry of education. The board of deacons shall act as the school board and shall hear all matters and disputes that may arise out of the ministry of education and shall advise the pastor accordingly. All recommendations of the board of deacons shall be submitted to the pastor for final approval prior to becoming effective. The board of deacons may create and recommend to the pastor school policies for governing the ministry of education consistent with the provisions herein.

ARTICLE 8—ORDINATION

SECTION 8.01—ORDINATION QUALIFICATIONS

Any man who is a member of this church or its mission churches, who gives evidence of a genuine call of God into the work of the ministry and possesses the qualifications stated in 1 Timothy 3:1–7 and Titus 1:6–9, may be ordained as a minister of the Gospel.

SECTION 8.02—ORDINATION PROCEDURE

(A) Upon a conference with the pastor and after the pastor has approved the candidate for ordination, the pastor shall call a council to examine and pass on the qualification of the candidate. The ordination council shall consist of the board of deacons and of ordained ministers of like faith invited by the pastor to participate in the examination.

(B) If the ordination council finds the candidate worthy of ordination, the ordination council may ordain the candidate on behalf of the church.

(C) The pastor and the deacons shall arrange for the ordination service.

ARTICLE 9—INDEMNIFICATION

SECTION 9.01—ACTIONS SUBJECT TO INDEMNIFICATION

The church may indemnify any person who was or is a party or is threatened to be made a party to any threatened, pending or completed action, suit, or proceeding; whether civil, criminal, administrative, or investigative, including all appeals (other than an action by or in the right of the church) by reason of the fact that the person is or was a pastor, deacon, officer, employee, or agent of the church, against expenses, including attorneys' fees, judgments, fines, and amounts paid in settlement actually and reasonably incurred by him in connection with the action, suit, or proceeding; and if that person acted in good faith and in a manner he reasonably believed to be in or not opposed to the best interests of the church and, with respect to any criminal action or proceeding, had no reasonable cause to believe his conduct was unlawful. The termination of any action, suit, or proceeding by judgment, order, settlement, conviction, or on a plea of *nolo contendere* or its equivalent, shall not, of itself, create a presumption that the person did not act in good faith and in a manner that he reasonably believed to be in or not opposed to the best interests of the church and, with respect to any criminal action or proceeding, had no reasonable cause to believe that his or her conduct was unlawful.

SECTION 9.02—EXPENSES SUBJECT TO INDEMNIFICATION

To the extent that a pastor, deacon, officer, employee, or agent has been successful on the merits or otherwise in defense of any action, suit, or proceeding referred to in this Article, or in defense of any claim, issue, or matter in that action, suit, or proceeding, he or she may be indemnified against expenses, including attorneys' fees, actually and reasonably incurred by him or her in connection with the action, suit, or proceeding.

SECTION 9.03—LIMITATIONS OF INDEMNIFICATION

Any indemnification made under this Article may be made by the church only as authorized in the specific case on a determination that indemnification of the pastor, deacon, officer, employee, or agent is proper in the circumstances because he has met the applicable standard of conduct set forth in Section 1 of this Article. The determination shall be made (a) by a majority vote of a quorum consisting of the pastor and deacons who were not and are not parties to or threatened with the action, suit, or proceeding; (b) if the described quorum is not obtainable or if a majority vote of a quorum of disinterested deacons so directs, by independent legal counsel in a written opinion; or (c) by a majority vote of the members of the church.

SECTION 9.04—TIMING OF INDEMNIFICATION

Expenses of each person seeking indemnification under this Article, may be paid by the church as they are incurred, in advance of the final disposition of the action, suit, or proceeding, as authorized by the board of deacons in the specific case, on receipt of an undertaking by or on behalf of the pastor, deacon, officer, employee, or agent to repay the amount if it is ultimately determined that he or she is not qualified to be indemnified by the church.

SECTION 9.05—EXTENT OF INDEMNIFICATION

The indemnification provided by this Article shall be deemed to be discretionary unless otherwise required as a matter of law or under any agreement or provided by insurance purchased by the church, both as to action of each person seeking indemnification under this Article in his official capacity and as to action in another capacity while holding that office, and may continue as to a person who has ceased to be a pastor, deacon, officer, employee, or agent and may inure to the benefit of the heirs, executors, and administrators of that person.

SECTION 9.06—INSURANCE

The church may purchase and maintain insurance on behalf of any person who is or was a pastor, deacon, officer, employee, or agent of the church against any liability asserted against him and incurred by him in that capacity, or arising out of his status in that capacity, whether or not the church would have the power to indemnify him against liability under the provisions of this Article.

ARTICLE 10—COMMITTEES

SECTION 10.01—STANDING COMMITTEES

The pastor (or the board of deacons if the office of pastor is vacant) shall appoint standing committees and designate a chairperson for each standing committee and, except when otherwise specifically provided in these bylaws, shall determine the membership of each standing committee. In addition to the discipline committee, the pastor may appoint other standing committees as he deems appropriate.

SECTION 10.02—SPECIAL COMMITTEES

The board of deacons, with expressed consent of the pastor, may create special committees to provide the board with advice and information regarding matters submitted to the committee by the board for consideration. The committee shall have no authority to act on behalf of the corporation. The members of the committee shall be chosen by a majority vote of the board of deacons and shall serve solely at the pleasure of the board of deacons. The special committee shall be subject to the control and direction of the board of deacons at all times. The pastor may also appoint such committees within the board of deacons at his discretion to fulfill needs for additional oversight in particular areas of the church's ministry.

ARTICLE 11—INNER ORGANIZATIONS

Every organization or society within this church will be an integral part of the church and not an entity in itself. Each such organization or society shall have as its aims and objectives that of assisting the church in discharging the obligations and responsibilities that have been imposed upon it, rather than having different aims and objectives, which commonly act as divisive forces. The pastor may reside over all such organizations and societies, and he may develop additional organizations and societies as the need arises. The following is a partial list of such organizations and societies, which is not to be considered inclusive due to the growth of the church and dynamic methods governed by the purposes set forth in Section 1.02:

1. Baptist Boys Club
2. Bookstore
3. Bus Ministry
4. Cactus Kids Club
5. Joy Club
6. Lancaster Baptist School
7. Saturday Bible School

8. Sunday School
9. Tape and Video Ministry
10. Daily in the Word Publications, Radio, and Internet Ministry
11. Striving Together Publications
12. West Coast Baptist College
13. Buckets and Bows
14. Tools and Ties
15. Hospitality Team
16. Usher Ministry
17. Reformers Unanimous

ARTICLE 12—DESIGNATED CONTRIBUTIONS

From time to time the church, in the exercise of its religious, educational, and charitable purposes, may establish various funds to accomplish specific goals. Contributors may suggest uses for their contributions, but all suggestions shall be deemed advisory rather than mandatory in nature. All contributions made to specific funds or otherwise designated shall remain subject to the exclusive control and discretion of the pastor and the board of deacons. No fiduciary obligation shall be created by any designated contribution made to the church other than to use the contribution for the general furtherance of any of the purposes stated in Section 1.02.

ARTICLE 13—BINDING ARBITRATION

SECTION 13.01—SUBMISSION TO ARBITRATION

Believing that lawsuits between believers are prohibited by Scripture, all members of this church agree to submit to binding arbitration any matters which cannot otherwise be resolved, and expressly waive any and all rights in law and equity to bringing any civil disagreement before a court of law, except that judgment upon the award rendered by the arbitrator may be entered in any court having jurisdiction thereof.

SECTION 13.02—NOTICE OF ARBITRATION

In the event of any dispute, claim, question, or disagreement arising out of or relating to these bylaws or any other church matter, the parties shall use their best efforts to settle such disputes, claims, questions, or disagreement as befits Christians. To this effect, they shall consult and negotiate with each other in good faith and, recognizing their mutual interests not to disgrace the name of Christ, seek to reach a just and equitable solution. If they do not reach such solution within a period of sixty (60) days, then upon notice by either party to the other, disputes, claims, questions, or differences shall be finally settled by arbitration as described in section 13.01, above, and such Procedures for Arbitration as are adopted pursuant to Section 13.04, below.

SECTION 13.03—LIMITATIONS ON ARBITRATION DECISIONS

(A)   Should any dispute involve matters of church discipline, the arbitrators shall be limited to determining whether the procedures for church discipline as outlined under Section 3.04, were followed.

(B)   Should any dispute involve the removal from office of the pastor or any church officer, the arbitrators shall be limited to determining whether the procedures set forth in Section 3.04 were followed.

SECTION 13.04—ARBITRATION PROCEDURES

The Procedures for Arbitration shall be as adopted by the pastor and the board of deacons.

ARTICLE 14—GOVERNMENT

SECTION 14.01—INDEPENDENCE OF THE CHURCH

This church shall be an independent body of baptized believers. The government of this church shall never be subject to the control of any other ecclesiastical body, and no denominational or associational representatives shall ever sit in judgment over its affairs. (Ephesians 1:22–23, 4:15–16, 5:23; Colossians 1:18, 2:10)

SECTION 14.02—COOPERATION WITH OTHER CHURCHES

The church may fellowship and may cooperate with other churches for the furtherance of the Gospel when such shall be wholly in accordance with the Scriptures, but no rules, regulations, or commitments shall be made to such bodies which call for more than voluntary action on the part of the church. (1 Corinthians 8:1–2)

ARTICLE 15—FINANCE

SECTION 15.01—SCRIPTURAL GIVING

Scriptural giving is an expression of love for the Lord Jesus Christ; therefore, the church shall be sustained by voluntary and free-will offerings uninfluenced by any consideration of material or worldly reward. Tithes and offerings brought into the general treasury of the church is the only method of finance found in the Scriptures; therefore, it shall be the duty of the members to bring their tithes and offerings into the general treasury of the church. (1 Corinthians 16:2; 2 Corinthians 9:7)

SECTION 15.02—MISSIONS

Missions will be supported by the Faith Promise Plan of giving explained each year during the annual Missions and Stewardship Conference.

SECTION 15.03—FINANCE COMMITTEE

The Finance Committee shall be comprised of men selected from the deacons. It shall be their responsibility to act as guardian of the church's financial interest. In the same spirit, as all other committees, they shall assist the pastor and help him expedite any matters involved in the church's official interest, and they shall work in concert with the financial administrator.

SECTION 15.04—TAX-EXEMPT PROVISIONS

(A)   Private Inurement: No part of the net earnings of the church shall inure to the benefit of or be distributable to its members, trustees, officers, or other private persons, except that the church shall be authorized and empowered to pay reasonable compensation for the services rendered and to make payments and distributions in furtherance of the purposes set forth in Section 1.02 hereof. (1 Timothy 3:2–3, 8, 5:17–18; Mark 12:17; 1 Corinthians 9:7–14; Galatians 6:6)

(B)   Political Involvement: No substantial part of the activities of the church shall be the carrying on of propaganda or otherwise attempting to influence legislation. The church shall not participate in, or intervene in (including the publishing or distribution of statements) any political campaign on behalf of any candidate for public office.

(C)   Dissolution: Upon the dissolution of the church, the trustees shall, after paying or making provision for payment of all the liabilities of the church, dispose of all assets of the church to such organization or organizations organized and operated exclusively for religious purposes as shall at the time qualify as an exempt organization or organizations under Section 501(c)(3) of the Internal Revenue Code of 1986 (or the corresponding provision of any future United States Internal Revenue Law), as the trustees shall determine. Assets may be distributed only to organizations which agree with the church's Statement of Faith.

(D) Racial Nondiscrimination: The church shall have a racially nondiscriminatory policy and, therefore, shall not discriminate against members, applicants, students, and others on the basis of race, color, or national or ethnic origin. (Matthew 11:28; John 3:16; 2 Peter 3:9; 1 John 2:2)

(E) Limitation of Activities: Notwithstanding any other provision of these bylaws, the church shall not, except to an insubstantial degree, engage in any activities or exercise any powers that are not in furtherance of the purposes stated in Section 1.02.

SECTION 15.05—FISCAL YEAR

The fiscal year of the church shall begin January 1st and end December 31st.

ARTICLE 16—AMENDMENTS

These bylaws may be revised or amended by a majority vote of the members present and voting at any regular church administration meeting, provided that said revision or amendment has been submitted in writing and announced from the pulpit fourteen (14) days before the vote is taken.

ADOPTION

These bylaws were adopted by a two-thirds majority vote of the members present and voting at a duly called meeting of the church in which a quorum was present.

These bylaws supersede any other bylaws of Lancaster Baptist Church.

_____	_____
Date	Pastor (President)
_____	_____
Date	Secretary

First Corinthians 6:1–8 warns Christians of the loss to the testimony of Christ when Christians bring each other to court. The following addendum to our church constitution provides an alternate source for arbitration between Christian brothers.

PROCEDURES FOR ARBITRATION

SECTION 1—SCOPE OF ARBITRATION

The parties must, prior to the selection of arbitrators, agree to the scope of the matters to be considered by the arbitrators. In doing so the parties must conduct themselves with the utmost courtesy as befits believers in Jesus Christ. If the parties cannot agree upon the scope of the dispute for arbitration, the scope shall be determined by the arbitrators.

SECTION 2—SUBMISSION TO ARBITRATION

(A)   The parties, as Christians, believing that lawsuits between Christians are prohibited by Scripture, and having agreed, according to Article 13 of the church bylaws, to submit disputes to binding arbitration, and to waive any legal right to take the dispute to a court of law, will refer and submit any and all disputes, differences, and controversies whatsoever within the agreed scope of arbitration to a panel of three arbitrators, to be selected as follows:

1.   All arbitrators must be born-again Christians of good reputation in the community and who affirm the church's Statement of Faith in its entirety.

2.   Each party shall submit a list of three proposed arbitrators to the other party, and the other party will choose one of the three proposed arbitrators to serve on the panel.

3.   The third arbitrator will be selected by mutual agreement of the other two arbitrators.

4.   In selecting the arbitrators, each party shall act in good faith in choosing Christian arbitrators who have no prior knowledge of the facts leading up to the dispute, are not related to or close friends with the

selecting party, and who will act impartially and with fundamental fairness.

5.   No arbitrator may be an attorney.

6.   No arbitrator may be employed or ever have been employed by, or under the authority of, either party or any other arbitrator.

7.   The arbitrators will be selected as soon as possible but no later than 30 days after the parties have agreed to the scope of the arbitration.

8.   The arbitration will be held at a neutral site agreed to by the arbitrators.

(B)   The arbitrators shall, subject to the provisions of these procedures, arbitrate the dispute according to the terms of these procedures, the Bible as interpreted by the church's Statement of Faith, and any applicable church documents.

(C)   Each party may be represented by counsel throughout the process at the party's own expense. Discovery will be allowed as needed, as determined in the discretion of the arbitrators. Formal rules of evidence shall not apply.

SECTION 3—TERMS AND CONDITIONS OF ARBITRATION

(A)   The arbitrators shall have full power to make such regulations and to give such orders and directions, as they shall deem expedient in respect to a determination of the matters and differences referred to them.

(B)   The arbitrators shall hold the arbitration hearing as soon as possible, but no later than thirty (30) days after the selection of the third arbitrator.

(C) There shall be no stenographic record of the proceedings, and all proceedings shall be closed to the media and any other individuals not directly involved in the proceedings.

(D) Normally, the hearing shall be completed within three (3) hours. The length of the hearing, however, may be extended by the arbitrators in their discretion or an additional hearing may be scheduled by the arbitrators to be held promptly.

(E) There will be no post-hearing briefs.

(F) The arbitrators are to make and publish their award, in writing, signed by each of them concerning the matters referred, to be delivered to the parties no later than forty-eight hours from the conclusion of the hearing, unless otherwise agreed by the parties. The arbitrators may, in their discretion, furnish an opinion.

SECTION 4—CONDUCT AND RULES OF HEARING

(A) The arbitrators may, in their absolute discretion, receive and consider any evidence they deem relevant to the dispute, whether written or oral, without regard to any formal rules of evidence.

(B) The parties and their respective witnesses must, when required by the arbitrators, attend and submit to examination and cross-examination under oath as to all or any of the matters referred to in the proceedings and to produce and deposit with the arbitrators all or any evidence within their possession or control concerning such matters.

(C) If a party defaults in any respect referred to in Subsection 4.2, above, the arbitrators may proceed with the arbitration in their discretion as if no such evidence were in existence, insofar as it may be favorable to the party in default.

(D)   All presentations shall be controlled by the arbitrators. Any disputes regarding procedure shall be decided solely by the arbitrators.

SECTION 5—DUTIES OF ARBITRATORS

(A)   The arbitrators are to receive all evidence, prayerfully consider such evidence in an impartial manner, and render a decision which, based upon Scriptural principles, is fair to all parties.

(B)   The arbitrators have full power to order mutual releases to be executed by the parties, and either of the parties failing, such orders shall have the effect of a release, and may be duly acknowledged as such.

(C)   In the event that either party or a witness for either party shall fail to attend the arbitration hearing, after such written notice to such party as the arbitrators shall deem reasonable, the arbitrators may proceed in the absence of such party or witnesses without further notice.

SECTION 6—DECISION OF ARBITRATORS

(A)   It is preferred that the arbitrators reach a unanimous decision, but if a unanimous decision cannot be obtained, a majority decision will be accepted. The written decision of a majority of the arbitrators shall be final and binding on all parties, and judgment upon the award rendered by the arbitrators may be entered in any court having jurisdiction thereof. There is no appeal from the decision of the arbitrators.

(B)   The decision of the arbitrators is to be kept confidential by all parties for a period of one year. For purposes of these procedures, the church membership may be informed of the decision if the church or any church pastors, officers, trustees, employees, or board members were a party to the proceeding.

(C)   Should any party commence legal proceedings against another party with respect to the agreed scope of the dispute or the binding decision of the arbitrators, with the exception of an action to enforce the decision of the arbitrators, that party shall pay to the other party all expenses of said proceedings, including reasonable attorneys' fees. In the event it becomes necessary for one party to commence legal proceedings to enforce the decision of the arbitrators, the non-prevailing party must bear all of the costs of the said proceedings, including reasonable attorneys' fees.

SECTION 7—PARTIES TO COOPERATE

No party shall unreasonably delay or otherwise prevent or impede the arbitration proceedings. No party will involve the news media in the dispute in any way. No party shall publicize the dispute in any way to anyone not a party to the proceedings, except as permitted by the arbitrators and except that a party may disclose the proceedings of this arbitration to his or her spouse, legal counsel, accountants, insurance carrier, and as otherwise required by law.

SECTION 8—COSTS AND EXPENSES

Each party shall pay his or her own costs and expenses related to presenting the party's case to the arbitrators. The costs of the arbitration, including any fees for the arbitrators is to be shared equally by both parties.

SECTION 9—COMMANDMENTS

These Procedures for Arbitration may be revised or amended by a majority vote of the board of deacons present and voting at any regular board meeting.

SECTION 10—ADOPTION

(A) These Procedures for Arbitration were adopted by a majority vote of the board of deacons at which a quorum was present.

(B) These Procedures for Arbitration supersede any other Procedures for Arbitration previously adopted by the board of deacons, if any exist.

_____   _____

Date Approved   Secretary

Visit us online

strivingtogether.com

wcbc.edu

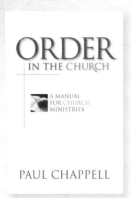
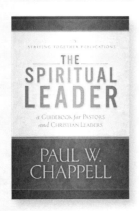

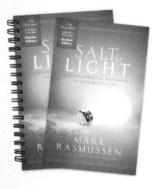